Long-Distance
Hiking

Long-Distance Hiking

Dan Feldman

STACKPOLE
BOOKS

Published by
STACKPOLE BOOKS
5067 Ritter Road
Mechanicsburg, PA 17055
www.stackpolebooks.com

Printed in the United States

First edition

10 9 8 7 6 5 4 3 2 1

Illustrations by Taina Litwak
Cover photo taken in the Bob Marshall Wilderness of Montana by the author

Library of Congress Cataloging-in-Publication Data

Feldman, Dan.
    Long-distance hiking / Dan Feldman.
        pages   cm
    Includes bibliographical references and index.
    ISBN-13: 978-0-8117-1227-9 (pbk.)
    ISBN-10: 0-8117-1227-3 (pbk.)
    1. Hiking. I. Title.
GV199.5.F45   2013
796.51—dc23
                                                                        2013004453

To April

Contents

Acknowledgments

My deepest gratitude extends to the delightful people who helped shepherd this book from its woebegone infancy to its rebellious teen years. Here's to old age: Mark Bailey, Kathryn Beaumont, Mary Beth Feldman, Barney Mann, April Robinson, and Judith Schnell.

The research for this book was conducted with the kind generosity of the Blueberry Patch Hostel in Hiawassee, Georgia, Hiker Heaven in Agua Dulce, California, Drakesbad Guest Ranch in Chester, California, and the AT and PCT hikers of 2011.

Introduction

I first thought about writing this book during a thru-hike of the Pacific Crest Trail (PCT) in 2007. I was solo hiking at the time, but my path would periodically cross that of two fellow hikers named Captain America and Billy Goat. Before beginning the PCT, they had finished a winter/spring hike of the Florida Trail. Billy Goat, who has hiked over 32,000 miles in his lifetime and was just a few years shy of 70, was having problems.

The long, hot road walks of the Florida Trail had wreaked havoc on Billy Goat's feet, causing pain with nearly every step. When we first met on the trail outside Mt. Laguna, Billy Goat attributed the pain to a pinched nerve between the balls of his feet but planned to continue walking to see if the softer ground of the PCT would let the nerve pain subside on its own. However, when we crossed paths again, this time high in the San Jacintos, Captain America and Billy Goat were having a hard time making progress together as Billy Goat's pain had not improved. He wasn't sure if he'd be able to continue on the PCT, and the two were discussing leaving the trail so that Billy Goat could take care of his feet.

Since I'm a physical therapist, I took a look at Billy Goat's shoes and found that they had very little support along the arch. This was causing his foot to flatten out too much, aggravating the pinched nerve. Since we were at least a day or two from a road and a shoe store, I improvised a temporary arch support for Billy Goat using a knife, a few pieces of my foam ground pad, and some tape (see page 125 for step-by-step instructions).

The support was intended to relieve the pinching and hold Billy Goat over until he could get to a sporting goods store, but it worked so well that he skipped the store and stuck with the trail-made version. When I ran into the companions later on, in Big Bear, Billy Goat told me he was still using the support design and had fabricated one of his own when the one I made wore out. It made me happy to know that a simple fix was enough to let Billy Goat continue on the PCT. I suspected that many people like

Billy Goat have gotten frustrated and abandoned a hike when all that was needed was a basic adjustment or two.

As I recall preparing for my PCT hike that year, I remember having read plenty of how-to books about backpacking, but I didn't find much information about managing the practical on-trail problems encountered on a hike as long as the 2,655-mile PCT. These problems extend far beyond just carrying the right gear and making sure that it works (although this helps). So I set out to write this book.

Long-distance hiking is my absolute favorite pastime, and I think it's one of the most thrilling and fulfilling adventures available to everyday people in modern times. The thrill of long-distance hiking lies not only in the excitement of being outdoors, but also the journey itself. In contrast to a day of fishing, a weekend of hunting, or even a week of backpacking where trips usually end back at the car with hot showers waiting at home, a long-distance hike is truly an exodus from modern life. On hikes that span several months, the journey becomes, just for a while, a brand-new lifestyle with a whole new set of priorities. Weather, shelter, physical and mental health, and basic nutrition become foremost in the minds of all long-distance hikers, no matter what they did before the journey.

Long-distance hiking is a journey by the simplest means possible: on foot. Following a trail for thousands of miles that might cross major mountain ranges or state and even national boundaries is a major personal achievement—one that can't be taken away. Some of the most vivid and happy memories I have come from long-distance hikes.

Long-distance hiking is remarkably accessible. The graph on page xiii shows that anyone, from a child to a retiree, can be a long-distance hiker. Of course, one must acquire gear, save money, and arrange time away from work and family (admittedly not easy steps), but otherwise there are few barriers to long-distance hiking. Aspiring hikers don't need to be athletes or even be in good shape! No guides, agents, training courses, certifications, classes, sponsors, or elaborate itineraries are needed. Prior experience is optional. My first overnight backpacking trip ever was my 2002 southbound Appalachian Trail (AT) thru-hike.

As wonderful and exciting as long-distance hiking is, it is also true that each year thousands of people set out with the intention of completing a long-distance hike only to fail. According to the Appalachian Trail Conservancy, the completion rate for attempted AT single-season thru-hikes from 2003 through 2008 ranged from 17 percent to 30 percent. Official statistics are not kept for the PCT, but best estimates place the single-season

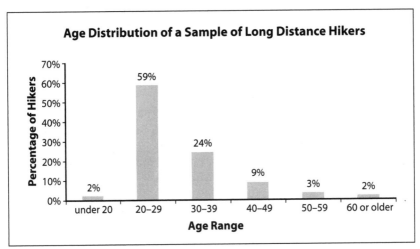

Survey by the author of 87 random hikers who thru-hiked the PCT or AT in 2011.

completion rate somewhere around 50 percent. These numbers are disappointing. There are lots of reasons for abandoning a long-distance hike: injury, family emergencies and commitments, bad weather, finances, boredom, misperceptions, and illness. Certainly some of these reasons are unavoidable. On the other hand, I believe that with the right body of knowledge, many failed attempts can be prevented.

The purpose of this book is to help aspiring long-distance hikers succeed. While everyone's idea about success is a little different, I define success in long-distance hiking as not only meeting a mileage or a destination goal, but also in having an experience that is positive and personally fulfilling. There are plenty of informative books that have been published about hiking, but not many have been written about hiking for hundreds or even thousands of miles and for months at a time. Lots of books and guides have been written about specific trails and about the gear you need for a long-distance hike, but few consider the on-trail skills that are so important to long-distance hiking, not only from a technical standpoint, but also from a psychological and practical standpoint. While this book does discuss gear and makes frequent reference to the Appalachian, Pacific Crest, and Continental Divide Trails, it is about neither gear nor specific trails. Choosing proper gear and being familiar with the ins and outs of trail logistics is only a small piece of what a long-distance hiker needs to be successful. Just as important is a hiker's ability to stay sharp in stressful or uncomfortable circumstances, to choose the right types of foods, to

In these pages, you'll find information from surveys that were completed in 2011 and asked current-year thru-hikers about their experiences. The surveys were distributed and compiled by the author. Three sets of paper surveys were placed at the following trail locations:

- The Blueberry Patch (mile 68, Appalachian Trail)
- Hiker Heaven (mile 454, Pacific Crest Trail)
- Drakesbad Guest Ranch (mile 1,354, Pacific Crest Trail)

Respondents to the paper surveys were invited to complete an online survey during the winter of 2011–12. I received 225 responses to the paper surveys and 120 responses to the online survey.

recognize boredom or a negative frame of mind, and, like Billy Goat, to manage a wound or injury. These skills are vital to the success of all long-distance hikers and make up the core content of this book.

I hope the information in this book provides you with valuable insight and perspective on what it takes to succeed at long-distance hiking. Most of all, I hope that your next trip will be one of the most fantastic adventures of your life.

1

Diet

It's No Fun Being Hungry

The hungriest I've ever felt was while hiking along the northernmost 261 miles of PCT in 2007. For the entire trail since Mexico, I had been resupplying about every 5 or 6 days and was rarely hungry as my diet consisted of calorie-dense, high-carbohydrate and high-fat foods like mac and cheese, candy bars, pastas with olive oil, and a super-filling breakfast of granola, Carnation Instant Breakfast, dry milk, and instant coffee.

When I got to northern California, I began sharing camp each night with Optimist and Stopwatch, an ambitious marathon-running couple from West Virginia affectionately known along the trail as Team Sherpa. With a few exceptions, Sherpa's hiking style involved passing up all resupply points that were more than a mile off the trail. On the PCT, which passes through a grand total of three developed towns, this often meant long hauls without resupply. Sherpa sometimes looked ridiculous coming out of a resupply with backpacks laden with untold quantities of food in preparation for the next several hundred miles of straight hiking. Add to this group a grizzled Canadian adventure racer named NoCar,

True to his word, NoCar finished the entire PCT without getting into a car. You can read his journal at http://www.trailjournals.com/nocar.

who had declared at the beginning of the trail that he would not set foot in a car until he reached Canada. This naturally limited his resupply options as well. The four of us camped together for several weeks, often exchanging tales of trail adventure and bravado. NoCar would grumble about the sometimes-illogical PCT, which would mindlessly switchback down ridges to roads far away from towns, forcing him to blaze a route of his own down arcane forest roads and bush in order to resupply. Camping together at night, we liked to discuss the problem of Washington, a state with few accessible resupply points for the Sherpa-NoCar way of travel. We ended up devising a plan called the *grand finale*, which was to hike from Snoqualmie Pass to Manning Park in Canada, a distance of 261 miles, without resupply. After weeks of camping with Sherpa and NoCar, I had been effectively brainwashed and convinced that the Sherpa-NoCar way of doing things was *the* best way to enjoy my remaining wilderness experience, and I looked forward to the challenge of the grand finale.

I began preparing when I arrived in Cascade Locks, the northernmost PCT town in Oregon. Sherpa and NoCar were a day or two ahead of me at that point, so I was on my own. I stayed at the home of my cousin Ross and his family in the nearby wind-surfing mecca of Hood River. Ross was kind enough to take me to the Portland REI to stock up on food, which I then repackaged and mailed to a motel at the I-90 rest stop in Snoqualmie Pass, Washington. Because I had been getting tired of eating my usual hiker food, I decided to switch my diet and stock up on "the good stuff," namely the high-end freeze-dried dinners that thru-hikers typically consider over-budget and under-calorie. I loaded up on beef stew, sweet and sour pork, hot apple cobbler, and other food that seemed downright mouth-watering at the time. I was determined to eat well on my last days of PCT hiking.

I arrived at Snoqualmie Pass in good shape, looking forward to picking up my box of freeze-dried goodies. After an afternoon of rest at the motel, I filled my pack to the brim in preparation for 9½ days of straight Washington wilderness. I headed off into the Alpine Lakes Wilderness the next day. The weight of the pack was definitely burdensome over the first days, but I gladly ate the weight down and by the fourth day my pack was back to a manageable size. The problem was, however, that with 5½ days to go I was beginning to get hungry. Meals would satisfy me in the short term, but hunger pangs would start several hours after a meal, prodding me to consume more food than I had. By the time I rounded the west side of Glacier Peak, bushwhacking and scrambling through a storm-battered section of PCT, I was completely famished. I remember waking up one night feeling so hungry that I was forced to tear into a snack for the next day ($0.99 bag of Cheetos) like a wild animal in order to sleep without my stomach growling.

The next morning, determined to push on and stick with the plan, I grudgingly hiked across the access road to Stehekin and on into North Cascades National Park. By skipping the road, I was missing out on the best bakery on the entire trail in the name of the Sherpa-NoCar way and the challenge of hiking 261 PCT miles without a stop. The ranger stationed at the road crossing mercifully offered me two apples, which I gratefully inhaled. But my hunger raged on. With a few days to go until I reached Canada, I was ready to throw in the towel and hitch into town, accepting a less-than-grand finale in return for not resorting to scrounging for grubs under stumps or cannibalizing the next unsuspecting hiker.

Leaving camp on the morning of my eighth day, I nearly ran straight into Jen. Jen was solo hiking from Walker Pass to Canada on the PCT and had been about half a day or so ahead of me through the entire state of Washington. As I passed Stehekin, I got ahead of her, literally, by a few minutes. I was very happy to see Jen. Not only was she the first thru-hiker I had seen in Washington, but she was also a potential source of extra food. She pledged a few Clif Bars. Glad to have a hiking partner for my entry into Canada and an emergency food source, I decided not to go into town and instead made a plan to beg food off section hikers going back to their cars on Labor Day weekend. The plan worked well. I scored bagels, nuts, candy, and any other types of food hikers were willing to give up for the sake of a starving thru-hiker so close to Canada. (I ended up with a lot of PowerBars!) I finished, but I learned a valuable lesson about diet.

By switching from boring pasta with olive oil to the delicious, but calorie-deficient freeze-dried foods, I set myself up for a long, hungry section of trail. True to my initial perusing of the nutrition labels, most of the freeze-dried foods I chose had a high calorie and carbohydrate count per serving. What I overlooked, however, were the total number of servings in each pouch, which was often insufficient. For example, the beef stew meal I packed contained a whopping 480 calories per serving.

> Of course, an obvious alternate criticism is that perhaps I shouldn't have tried to hike 9½ days in northern Washington with a mid-volume pack. But what fun is that?

Not bad. The problem was, each pouch contained only a single serving, leaving me hungry for more food afterward. Relying on one of these types of meals for my dinner each night caused my calorie deficiency to add up quickly. Before getting food donations from other hikers, my average calorie intake was 3,400 calories per day. I should probably have been eating closer to 4,000 daily calories, given the rugged terrain and the long length of the haul. To achieve this level, I would have needed many more freeze-dried meals to ensure enough calories for 9½ days. Freeze-dried meals tend to be bulky, even when repackaged, so I couldn't even have fit that many in my pack. I should have stuck with my usual diet.

What to Expect on the Trail

Usually the first thing that comes to mind when thinking about food and long-distance hiking is hunger. You might have an image of a group of grubby, dusty people wolfing down triple-decker burgers and pints of ice cream at the local trail town diner. Why do hikers get so hungry? It's for the simple reason that carrying enough calories to hike from dawn to dusk through mountains and not be hungry is logistically quite difficult. Requirements for an 8-hour day of backpacking are in the range of 4,000 to 5,000 calories, depending on terrain, a person's pack weight, level of fitness, height, age, and body composition. Maintaining such a level of calorie intake without excessive contributions to pack weight requires a very specific selection of foods.

> The most public place to find thru-hikers pigging out might be the McDonalds on I-5 in Cajon Pass, California. The PCT runs right by these Golden Arches, and on any given day in May you'll find thru-hikers mixing with the regular crowd.

Distance hikers tend to suffer from a chronic shortage of calories, a problem that is compounded the longer the distance between resupply points. As an example of this compounding effect, imagine a hiker who needs 4,000 calories per day, but only carries 3,500. After one day, the 500-calorie deficit might not be noticeable, and the hiker probably still has extra calories stored up from eating in town. After five days, the deficit is

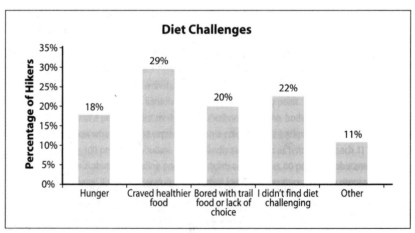

Eighty-five hikers who finished the AT or PCT in 2011 answered the question, "What was the most challenging aspect of your trail diet?"

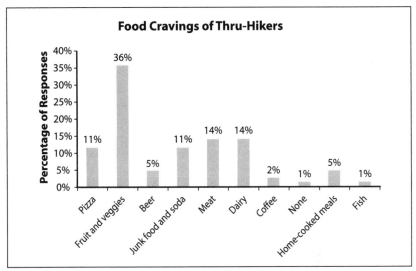

Eighty-two hikers who finished the AT or PCT in 2011 had a total of 87 responses.

at 2,000 calories, a half-day's worth of food. At nine days, the hiker may have lost some weight and will be short nearly a full day's worth of food and quite famished. This is how hiker hunger develops from a slow, but steady calorie deficiency between resupply stops across the time span of a long-distance hike.

While hunger is a prominent and well-talked-about feature of the long-distance hiking experience, thru-hikers don't always view being hungry as the most challenging aspect of trail diet. Indeed, many hikers found that their cravings for healthy food and being bored with usual trail food or lack of choice were more challenging to manage than being hungry on the trail. The wide variety of food cravings experienced by hikers illustrated in the graph helps to make this point. Some of the more interesting responses are listed below:

- Pizza, Taco Bell, sushi
- Fruits on the trail . . . cheeseburgers when in town
- Anything that could rot like fresh veggies
- Chocolate cheesecake, guys like meat and beer
- Lasagna, although Mountain House has a pretty good trail substitute!
- Arizona Iced Tea, beer, coffee, Olive Garden

- Full-course meals, freshly prepared foods
- Hot foods (didn't cook while on the trail), home-cooked meals, and pizza
- Oreos and Mocha Frappes
- Fresh fruit and vegetables, yogurt, fresh milk
- Fresh vegan food
- Lettuce
- Slushies
- Vegetable stir fry
- Real coffee
- After the first month, I didn't crave much. Before that, eggs and veggies.
- Red meat in the beginning, anything calorie-dense (sugar, mayonnaise, bread and butter) near the end
- Real home-cooked meals, not dehydrated foods
- Pizza, ice cream, and whiskey
- In the beginning, fresh fruits and veggies. By the end, anything with fat and salt
- Thai food

Like fingerprints, no two hikers have the same experience, and when it comes to diet, experiences vary significantly. The rest of this chapter is devoted to trail nutrition and a method for choosing trail food that takes some of the mystery out of the trail diet and addresses common food-related challenges that thru-hikers experience.

Trail Nutrition

Traditional nutrition guidelines tell us that a healthy diet consists of a moderate to low intake of fats, salts, and carbohydrates with an emphasis on grains, fresh fruits, and vegetables. On a long-distance hike, this gets flipped on its head. Foods loaded with carbohydrates and fat take priority because hikers need energy—lots of it. A diet of low- or no-fat foods will result in constant hunger after a few days on the trail. Fresh fruits, vegetables, and breads—while tasty—tend to be too heavy or bulky to carry in significant quantities and don't provide the caloric needs of day-in-and-day-out hiking.

This topic deserves a bit more explanation. Most people are familiar with the basic building blocks of nutrition: carbohydrates (carbs), lipids (fats), and proteins. In typical backpacking foods, carbs come in the form of pastas, rice, crackers, cereal, and beans and are an easy source of energy. Fats, often found in dairy products, nuts, and oils, are important for body insulation, skin, hair, cell function, and energy. Protein can be found naturally in beans, meat, fruits, cheese, and eggs. Protein supplies the body with essential amino acids, which are important for maintaining and building body tissue. The rest of the human diet is made up of vitamins and minerals, which help cells function.

For distance hiking, you can determine the relative importance of each nutrient from the speed at which the body can metabolize nutrients into energy and the quantity of energy a nutrient produces. All nutrients are able to supply the body with energy. Carbs and proteins provide 4 kilocalories of energy per gram and fats provide 9 kilocalories of energy per gram. However, fat and protein are much more complicated for the body to metabolize and take a longer time to yield their energy than carbs. Because of the speed at which they yield energy, carbs are the most important source of *short-term* energy for the body. Because long-distance hikers need an abundance of readily available energy to sustain a full day of walking, they need to eat a lot of carbohydrates. Fats yield more than double the energy of carbs, but take much longer to do so. Therefore fats are an important source of *long-term* energy for the body. Protein contributes as much energy as carbs, but takes much longer to do so. Over the long haul, the body needs the amino acids supplied by protein, but protein is not a ready source of energy.

Carbohydrates and fats are the most essential components of a long-distance hiker's diet. Together they supply large quantities of caloric energy for long days on the trail. Without sufficient quantities of these two nutrients, you'll become hungry and exhausted quickly, leading to an early exit from the trail. When planning a trail diet, keeping track of these nutrients in addition to total calories is important. It may seem like a boring, daunting task, but there is a fairly simple method, which I call the Achilles method, for organizing information about food that takes out a lot of the guesswork.

Choosing Trail Food: The Achilles Method

Before describing the Achilles method, I want to emphasize that long-distance hiking is not an exact science where one method of doing things is the only way of doing things. That type of thinking is never true in long-distance hiking and is certainly not in the spirit of this book. Food is one of those subjects (gear is another) where personal tastes and philosophies, even if they don't make a lot of sense, carry significant weight in terms of the overall enjoyment of the long-distance hiking experience. The Achilles method, rooted in basic nutritional science, feedback from long-distance hikers, and the belief that less pack weight is desirable, will work very well for many people, but it might not be too helpful for others. I am not presenting this method as the only way to choose food. So read on and decide if this method might be for you.

The Achilles method follows five steps, which are in order of importance:

1. Enjoy your food and have fun!

While not very scientific, this first step is the most important. For all but a few diehards, food eaten on a long-distance hike should be enjoyable and varied. There may be certain foods that you discover in the planning process that seem like "superfoods." Please don't fall into the trap of buying cases of these foods ahead of time, even if you're really excited about eating them. The monotony of eating the same thing every day or the displeasure of eating food that doesn't taste good, regardless of its nutritional content or weight advantage, can make hiking a real slog. If you want to test this theory, think of your favorite food (mmm, lobster), and then eat it every day for seven days and see if you're not sick of it.

> My favorite trail comfort foods? Cold beer, frozen strawberries (sweetened), and avocado.

The Achilles method is a numbers-driven approach, but the numbers mean nothing if you're not having fun and enjoying the foods you eat. You might not like everything you eat every day, but make sure you're packing some comfort foods that make you happy and that you can look forward to, even if they don't fall into any of the categories in the following steps.

2. Locate foods with high calorie densities.

Calorie density (CD) in food is defined as the number of calories per unit of weight and is the first thing I always look at when choosing food. This is because foods with high calorie densities pack the most energy for what they weigh, which is what you want on a long-distance hike. A food's CD can be calculated by simply looking at the nutrition label and doing some basic math: Multiply the number of calories per serving by the number of servings in the package, and then divide by the weight of the package.

> The minimum calorie density for backpacking foods is one of those topics that diehards like to debate. Some prefer a cutoff at 120 calories per ounce. I'm happy with 100.

Nutrition Facts	
Serving Size ½ Package	
Servings Per Container 2	
Amount Per Serving	
Calories 310 Calories from Fat 15	
	% Daily Value
Total Fat 2g	3%
Saturated Fat 0g	0%
Trans Fat 0g	
Cholesterol 25mg	9%
Sodium 1540mg	64%
Total Carbohydrates 56g	19%
Dietary Fiber 4g	16%
Sugars 9g	
Protein 20g	
Vitamin A 30% • Vitamin C 60%	
Calcium 15% • Iron 8%	

Nutrition Facts	
Serving Size ½ Package	
Servings Per Container 2	
Amount Per Serving	
Calories 310 Calories from Fat 15	
	% Daily Value
Total Fat 2g	3%
Saturated Fat 0g	0%
Trans Fat 0g	
Cholesterol 25mg	9%
Sodium 1540mg	64%
Total Carbohydrates 56g	19%
Dietary Fiber 4g	16%
Sugars 9g	
Protein 20g	
Vitamin A 30% • Vitamin C 60%	
Calcium 15% • Iron 8%	

Rice and Chicken

NET WT 6.4 OZ (182g)

The nutrition label on food packaging has all the information you need to use the Achilles method.

Here's an example: A package of freeze-dried rice and chicken contains 310 calories per serving. There are two servings per package, and the package weighs 182 grams. That's 2 x 310 calories ÷ 182 grams = 3.4 calories per gram. I consider 3.5 calories per gram (approx 100 calories per ounce) as a minimum CD value for food I'd take on a backpacking trip. Anything else, to me, seems too heavy for the number of calories it provides. The rice and chicken is a tad light on CD. If I really loved how it tasted, I'd probably bring it along.

> For simplicity, don't worry about the different types of carbs and fat; just use the total figures. The different types of carbs and fat are meaningful at microscopic levels, but long-distance hikers rarely have the time to parse them out. The Achilles method is designed to be quick.

3. Aim for a 3:2 ratio of carbs to fat.

In taking a look at some of the sample diets posted online by well-known long-distance hikers, total carbohydrate intake is usually around 1½ times the intake of fat. In my own experience, this seems to be about right, although it's not important to be dead-on precise. The carbs-to-fat (CTF) ratio represents the blend of carbs to fat in food and is also pretty easy to calculate: Look at the nutrition label and divide the total carbohydrate value by the total fat value. Taking our rice and chicken example: Total carbohydrates = 30g and total fat = 10g. 30g ÷ 10g = 3. This number is a bit high, indicating that the rice and chicken lacks fat and would perhaps benefit from adding a more fat-dense food like cheese.

Unlike calorie density, it's hard to find single foods with an ideal CTF ratio, so don't waste your time trying to hit the 3:2 mark for everything you pack. It's easier to look at CTF ratio over an entire outing (from one resupply point to the next), totaling all the food to be carried and coming up with a single net ratio. From there, food can be added as needed to bring the CTF ratio for the outing close to 3:2. See the worksheet at the end of this chapter for details.

4. Try to get close to 4,000 calories per day.

This is not as important if the amount of time between towns is just a few days. For hauls of 4 or 5 days, staying near 4,000 calories per day might help stave off hunger. For hauls longer than 5 days, especially over rough terrain, getting near or above the 4,000-calorie-per-day mark is more important for avoiding exhaustion and hunger. Remember my 9½-day journey at the end of the PCT? This was an example of not taking enough calories for a very long jaunt. I was in tip-top physical shape at this point in my thru-hike, and 3,400 calories per day was not enough.

Calories per day is another easy calculation: For each food item you're taking on an outing, take the number of calories per serving and multiply by the number of servings to get a total number of calories per food item. Next add all the food item totals together to get a total number of calories for the outing. Finally divide the total by the number of days on the outing to get the number of calories per day. The worksheet at the end of the chapter provides a user-friendly way of doing this.

5. Keep track of your salt intake.

While not a meaningful source of energy, salt is crucial for essential body functions such as sweating, conduction of nerve impulses, and fluid regulation. Salt is especially important in hot climates when a lot of it is lost through sweat. Under these conditions, it's important to pack a lot of salty foods and eat throughout the day. Thankfully, lots of calorie-dense foods like chips and crackers contain plenty of salt, so you usually do not need to make a major adjustment when following the Achilles method.

Those are the five steps. I've intentionally left out protein, a seemingly important nutrient. While I agree that protein is definitely important to long-distance hikers, it's not a high priority for the Achilles method for several reasons. First is that by eating calorie-dense foods that are high in carbs and fat, you usually consume sufficient amounts of protein at the same time. Second, because protein is not a main energy source, you can skimp on it while on the trail. You can make up protein deficits in town by binging on pizzas and burgers. Try to go for five days short on carbs and fat, however, and you'll pay the price. Protein is still important, just not as high a priority as carbs and fat.

The other things I've left out of the Achilles method are specific vitamins and minerals. First, like protein, many of the essential vitamins and minerals are consumed incidentally by following the Achilles method. Those that aren't, like vitamin C, can be consumed in town. If you're uneasy about being short on vitamin C or other vitamins, pack along a multivitamin. They're light and easy to carry. I recommend paying attention to vitamins and non-salt minerals only if you have a known chronic deficiency. A person with an iron deficiency, for example, should probably bring iron supplements.

There are a few other considerations to keep in mind when selecting backpacking food. First, make sure you can condense the food into a small space. A quality, lightweight backpack only has room for so much. Bulky, hard-to-pack items like boxes and pouches with a lot of air take up too much pack space. Most food can be repackaged or combined into baggies to eliminate bulky packaging. I like to do this with boxed food like Wheat Thins. For food already packaged in bags, like chips, I poke a tiny hole in the bag to let out the air and then roll up the bag and secure it with a rubber band.

Second, be sure to always browse the preparation instructions. Some food looks perfect for the trail, but requires additional ingredients or long cooking times. I've spent too many evenings sitting hungrily and waiting for certain brands of rice and beans to cook. Be aware that the cooking instructions on packaged food assume you are in a cozy, modern kitchen. Cook times in the backcountry, especially at high elevation, are usually longer than what is noted on the box. If you're going for rice and beans, look for instant or parboiled rice.

Ultimately, choosing food for a backpacking trip is a dance between food that packs the right nutritional punches and is light, easy to pack, efficient to prepare, varied, and enjoyable to eat. It's up to you to experiment and find your balance of foods that meet these criteria. The Achilles method sets the groundwork to do this, and the worksheet at the end of this chapter is a helpful tool. The method isn't perfect, but when I have a day in town to shop, I need an easy, quick, and reliable way to buy groceries so I can spend more of my town time relaxing with a beer! I use the Achilles method as a way of finding the foods that have the most of what's critical and pack the most energy for what they weigh. The Achilles method may take a little time to learn at first, but in time you'll be able to quickly identify foods that make the cut. To make the process even easier, see the list of common backpacking foods along with their calorie densities and nutritional info in the appendix.

> Once I packed along powdered Kool-Aid, only to discover at the end of a long, hot day on the trail that I needed to add sugar. I made the Kool-Aid without sugar, and it tasted nasty! It became useless weight until my next resupply.

Achilles Method Worksheet

Record all food to be taken between resupply points and calculate totals.

Use appendix 1 for values of common foods. "Quantity" refers to the amount of food you're planning on taking. It may be a whole box of something or just a single serving.

Food Description/Quantity	Total Calories in Quantity	Weight of Quantity (g)	Total Carbs (g) in Quantity	Total Fat (g) in Quantity
Sum Totals	A:	B:	C:	D:

Net Calorie Density (goal 3.5 cal/g or 100 cal/oz)

Total A ÷ Total B = _____

Net Carb/Fat Ratio (goal approx. 1.5)

Total C ÷ Total D = _____

Net Calories per Day (goal >4,000)

Total A ÷ number of days between resupply points = _____

Salty foods each day? ____y ____n

Variety of foods/comfort foods? ____y ____n

To calculate calories, carbs, or fat in a quantity: Multiply calories, carbs, or fat per serving by number of servings in quantity.

2

Water

Nothing is worse than being out of water, thirsty, and not knowing the location of the next reliable source. Thirst drives hikers to do things like drink from swampy puddles and cattle ponds. On the plus side, thirst also brings out bold ingenuity and generally improves skill in locating water.

I remember one evening on the CDT where my wife, April, and I had our ingenuity put to the test. We had the opportunity to fill our water bottles in the late afternoon, but looking ahead on the map it seemed as though there would be plenty of water where we planned to camp. So we drank a little, filled our bottles a little, and went on our way, planning to fill for the evening at one of the streams on the map.

As our trail turned from footpath to dirt road, we noticed that the streams we expected to encounter on our way to camp were either dry or mostly mud and cow swamp. We finished our water and as the shadows started to fall, we became progressively thirstier with no water to drink or cook with. We started to doubt that we'd find water before camp and decided that it was time to get creative.

As we happened to be on a dirt road in a scenic area, we were passed a few times by vehicles. Our first move, then, was to stop a vehicle and see if there was water on board. We eventually saw a white pickup bouncing down the road with a cloud of dust trailing, and I stepped partly into the road and held out my hand.

I think there's good etiquette to follow when asking for stuff. Don't just ask directly for whatever it is you want. It's rude. I like to start a conversation around what it is I'm interested in obtaining. Our conversation went like this:

"Hi, we're headed down the road to camp, are you guys from around here?"

"We're from the next town over."

"Oh, well, I was wondering if you knew if this road crosses water up ahead or if there's a stream nearby. We're really low on water."

"I'm not sure, but we've got a bottle of water here if you'd like it."

"Oh no, we'll find some water, I'm sure. You don't need to give us yours."

"Please, take our bottle; you look thirsty."

"OK, thanks a lot!"

Now as it turned out, we only got a liter from the truck. This quenched our thirst, but we'd need a lot more to make camp, so it was up to us to find water. We found a spot to camp near the side of the dirt road, and I took out the map and scanned the terrain. The map indicated that there might be a trickle of water about half a mile downhill. We had passed dry streams before, but looking out to where the water should be, we noticed a gently sloping gully lined with trees between two hills. Should be water there. April set up the tent, and I picked my way down the hillside, dodging cow patties along the way. In the gully, sure enough, was a stream. It was a small one and likely trampled by cattle, but it was water all the same. I picked a spot where water was flowing over a stick and filled up. It was a bit murky, but we filtered it, and it tasted great! We went to sleep with big smiles and plenty of water to drink.

Conventional wisdom for backcountry travel dictates that a hiker should carry enough water to stay regularly hydrated on the trail, and this holds true for distance hiking. It doesn't mean, however, that you need to carry copious amounts of water at all times.

Weighing 8.3 pounds per gallon (2.23 pounds/liter, 1kg/liter), water is one of the heaviest things a hiker can carry. Yet water is one of the most essential things a hiker (and everyone else) needs to survive.

A good water strategy permits adequate hydration throughout the day while minimizing the amount of water that you need to carry. You accomplish this by learning the skills to reliably identify and plan around water sources, understanding the effects of climate and terrain on thirst, and gaining an understanding about how your own body handles water.

Reliably Locate Water

Being able to reliably locate water is perhaps one of the most underappreciated skills in backpacking. It helps to have experience out on the trails, but if experience is lacking, common sense and practical thinking can go a long way. The key to identifying reliable water sources is cross-referencing.

The best way to end up thirsty on the trail is to rely on a single source of information for locating water. I once got stuck without water by choosing to camp based solely on the information on the map. My parents and I were making our way around the Three Sisters peaks in Oregon at the time, and I picked out a spot to camp near what was, on the map, a solid blue line, indicating a stream. We passed a rapid stream on our way up to the campsite and picked up just enough water to quench our thirst. When we got to our campsite for the night, that blue line on the map turned out to be a dry gully. I had to run three or four miles back to the stream to get us water for the night. Not too much fun.

Unless you know an area well, the best way to reliably locate water sources is to cross-reference. This means using multiple sources to confirm the presence of water. Sources can vary, but usually include at least two of the following:

- Guidebook
- Map/GPS
- Other hikers
- Locals
- Terrain features
- Internet hiker clubs and volunteers

Although maps give the most detail when it comes to water, the problem with solely relying upon a map is that water sources on maps are only as good as the last agency that updated them, and sometimes this means a U.S. Geological Survey done in the 1970s. Solely relying on a map or a GPS to locate water, especially in dry regions, can be a bad idea. Maps become exponentially more useful when cross-referenced with another published source. Examples include the Appalachian Long Distance Hikers Association's publication *Appalachian Trail Thru-Hikers' Companion* for the AT, or the online volunteer-maintained *Pacific Crest Trail Water Reports*. I found the latter to be extremely helpful on the PCT, where I was able to locate many off-map water sources and saved myself the hassle of carrying too much water. Other hikers, particularly those hiking in the opposite direction as you, can also be a valuable resource for cross-referencing water sources. Using additional sources will aid not only in establishing the reliability of a map, but they will also help in locating off-map water sources such as fire service caches and water left at trailheads by locals.

It's important to be a careful connoisseur of information, especially when using other people as a cross-reference. For instance, if a map and a well-respected guidebook indicate that a water source may be a little hard to find and an oncoming hiker says the source is dry or not even there, I'm inclined to stick with the guidebook and map, assuming the hiker didn't look hard enough. On the other hand, if a small, thin blue line labeled so-and-so "creek" on a map is identified as dry by a guidebook and confirmed dry by other hikers, I can pretty much bet on there being no water.

If you're stuck with just a map, as April and I were on the CDT, you're not completely out of luck as long as you have some skill in reading a map's topographical features. This is a valuable skill to learn for any trail, and I highly recommend anyone thinking about a distance hike learn the basics of map topography. Topography can often give big clues about where water should reliably be found. In general, water is less likely to occur along ridges or at high points on a map and more likely to be found along low points.

Visual identification of terrain features is another good way to potentially verify information on maps, or even to find water that might not have made it into a guidebook or map notation. A good way to use terrain to locate water is to think about where water should be. Is there a particularly dense growth of bushes or trees? Does the ground slope down somewhere? Gullies, low sloping points, animal pastures (if you are desperate), and strings of green foliage in an otherwise dry location often indicate the presence of water. Reedy plants growing on spongy land may eventually lead to a water source. In addition to using your eyes, it helps to use your ears. Water, unless it's in a stagnant pool, spring, or cistern, makes noise. Listen for it!

Finding water can be a messy adventure, but there's nothing more satisfying than hoisting a bag full of water and carrying it up to your partner when all hope had been lost. Whatever you do, don't give up just because water isn't right in front of you.

Make Adjustments and Carry What You Need

Once you can reliably find water, you need to consider the climate and terrain. Your body usually needs more water in steep terrain, where water is lost through sweating, high muscular force output, and higher rates of breathing. Hot and humid conditions may also lead to more sweating, thus placing a higher water demand on your body. Cold, dry, and flat climates draw on less of your body's water resources. Once you consider all of this, you can carry only the amount of water you need between reliable sources.

Reducing the amount of water you carry is one of the best ways to reduce pack weight. Even around reliable sources, too many hikers overload themselves with water for fear they're going to run out or to keep extra water around just in case. While always carrying extra water is not wrong, it's not a good way to save pack weight and space. Carrying the weight of extra water also is a catch-22—you increase your body's demand for water through increased muscular effort and sweating.

In cool, wet environments with abundant reliable water sources, such as the High Sierra Nevada on the PCT, you can often go without carrying any water at all, especially if your chosen method for purifying water doesn't involve long wait times.

Camping near water is another good way to cut down on water-based pack weight. On trails in the southwestern United States, where there are sometimes distances of 20 miles or more between natural water sources, planning to camp near water can make a huge difference in the amount of weight you need to carry each day. If you plan for a reliable water source at the end of the day, you can carry less water from the last source. While camping near water will keep needless weight out of the pack, it will sometimes mean hiking shorter days or longer days as a result, especially in dry sections. Those who prioritize big-mile days above everything else might elect to carry extra water.

Understand Your Body's Water Needs

Learn about how your own body handles water. Everyone handles water a little differently. Some folks get thirsty easily, some tend to sweat more or less than others. Understanding how your body handles water will allow you to judge how much water you need to carry.

A good way to judge your body's water needs is to look at how much water you have left when you arrive at a water source. Are you consistently arriving at water sources

> If you tend to sweat heavily and you're planning to hike in warm, humid conditions, do your best to wear light, breathable clothing to maximize air-cooling and cut down on water lost due to sweat.

with extra water on board? You might be overestimating your water needs. On the other hand, if you're consistently thirsty miles before a water source, you might want to carry a little more.

3
Gear

The subject of gear almost didn't make it into this book. Why? Because when it comes to the factors that influence the successful completion of a long-distance hike, gear is low on the list. Does it really matter whether you go with brand name X over brand name Y? The canister stove over the alcohol stove? No and yes. According to survey results, gear is not a reason for leaving the trail.

> Of the 120 thru-hikers who completed the 2011 online survey, 32 did not finish their hike. None of the 32 cited gear in their top three reasons for not finishing.

However, some thru-hikers do find gear to be one of the more challenging things to deal with on the trail. The graph shows that, in terms of overall difficulty, thru-hikers of 2011 who finished the trail and responded to the survey found gear to be as challenging as dealing with boredom, missing family or friends, and illness.

Common sense dictates that choosing the gear that is right for you can make life a lot easier on the trail. This chapter, then, deals with the problem of choice with the hopes that being able to make a more informed choice about gear will lead to fewer problems in the field and a happier hike.

This chapter does not explore every possible type of gear and the infinite choices associated with each. You won't find a discussion about

> Clothing is also important, and it is covered in the chapter on the elements.

trekking poles or compasses here. Rather, I'll discuss five types of gear that I think have the biggest influence over happiness on the trail: your choice of footwear, stove, water treatment, shelter, and sleeping bag.

This chapter provides basic decision-making guidelines. Despite what you might read about in magazines or hear from retailers and manufac-

Thru-Hikers Report the Most Challenging Aspects of Thru-Hiking

Eighty-four AT and PCT thru-hikers ranked the top three things they found to be most challenging about their trip. Not every hiker provided three choices, but all hikers picked a first choice.

turers, there's no single right answer when it comes to gear. Whether you choose a canister stove or an alcohol stove ultimately depends on the environment you'll be hiking through, your budget, the pros and cons associated with each technology, and perhaps most importantly, how all of the above relate to your style and priorities.

Footwear

Because they take more physical abuse than any other body part, your feet must be well taken care of, and choosing good footwear is part and parcel of a successful hike. Good footwear will reduce the risk of blisters or injury and protect the feet from the outside environment. Bad footwear will accomplish just one or none of these.

Good footwear doesn't necessarily need to keep the feet warm or dry. Many successful long-distance hikers are content to sacrifice occasional cold, wet feet for lighter, more breathable, and more comfortable shoes (more on this later in the chapter). Good footwear reduces the risk of blister formation, but it's not realistic to think that shoes can completely eliminate blister risk.

There's an expression in the world of physical therapy: When the foot hits the ground, everything changes. The expression emphasizes that the feet are the body's first point of impact with the ground. The rest of the actions the body takes can be seen as a reaction to what the foot does. If the foot has to twist or abnormally arrange itself in order to make the body feel stable inside a poorly fitting shoe, the ankle, knee, hip, and spine will have to make compensations as well.

If you're new to long-distance hiking, choosing the right footwear can be overwhelming. The amount of complex technology that goes into modern footwear manufacturing is extensive and choices for the consumer can take up an entire wall at an outfitter. This can make choosing good shoes seem impossible because of the variations in style, tread, construction, lacing, water resistance, cut, and so on.

In my experience, hikers eventually identify a manufacturer that makes the right shoe for them, some-

> I find that Salomon shoes fit me well. It's hard to explain exactly why, but they have just the right combination of structural elements that make my feet feel good on the trail.

times through a bit of trial and error. While finding the right footwear can be time consuming, when you've found that pair of shoes that make your feet feel great, you'll know that it's been a worthwhile process.

Essential considerations

Before setting off to shop for footwear, here are a few tips that will lower your chances of making a mistake:

If this is your first long-distance hiking trip, buy only one pair. Experienced hikers sometimes buy several pairs at once to save time and ensure that their favorite shoes will be available when their old ones fall apart. This is not my recommendation for first-timers for two reasons:

1. Footwear that fits perfectly in the store might not behave well on the trail. Veteran distance hikers know how a shoe performs on the trail, but first-timers might not.
2. It's not unusual for feet to increase in size on a long hike.

Buy shoes that are your size. Even though your feet will grow, swell, and sometimes feel cramped hiking day in and day out, the risks you take by buying shoes a half to a whole size larger are instability of the ankle and increased chance of blister formation through friction and smashing your toes at the end of the shoe during downhill hiking. Shoes will eventually loosen and expand with use.

Buy shoes with the socks you intend to wear. Don't go into the store wearing your office socks if you're not wearing office socks on the trail.

Don't buy online. If you want to buy online, be absolutely sure you have made the right choice. Paying a little extra in stores is worth being able to try on the shoe and work with an experienced store associate.

Waterproofing isn't essential. When hiking all day in the pouring rain, your feet will not stay dry, even with waterproof boots and rain pants. Don't waste your time and hard-earned money trying to build a footwear system that will keep water out at all costs. That said, it's nice to have footwear that incorporates water-resistant material like Gore-Tex. These shoes will be heavier and perhaps less breathable, but you'll have some protection from light rain and small, shallow puddles. For some hikers, myself included, the extra weight and cost for a shoe with Gore-Tex is worthwhile. For others, it's not. Now let's get down to what to look for when shopping for shoes.

Style

The first thing to decide on when you're shopping for footwear is what style you're looking for. A typical backpacking outfitter will stock two basic styles: boots and trail runners.

Most people know boots when they see them. For the purposes of this book, boots are any type of footwear, including "light hikers," that fully encloses the ankle. Boots used to be the norm for trail footwear. We were supposed to accept boots for their durability, weatherproofing, ankle protection, and, like a luxury SUV, the ability to trod across nearly any surface without noticing. In return for this, hikers were supposed to put up with wearing a pound or more of shoe on each foot and long break-in times. Over time and with the success some long-distance hikers were having in foregoing boots for plain, inexpensive sneakers, the trail runner evolved. The beauty of the trail runner was that it incorporated some of the rugged qualities of boots on a lightweight sneaker design, giving hikers the best of both worlds. You might hear some salespeople tell you that trail runners are nice for day hikes, but you'll need boots for serious distance. They are wrong. Among long-distance hikers today, boots are in the distinct minority.

It's easy to understand why boots are in the minority by exploring the so-called advantages of boots.

Durability. Well-made boots are indeed quite durable, but well-made trail runners hold up pretty well too. My Salomon trail runners lasted me about 1,300 miles on the PCT before they fell apart.

Rugged construction. Full leather uppers and thick, impenetrable soles are nice, but do you really need them for three-season backpacking? You're more apt to feel the ground beneath your feet in trail runners, but your feet will adapt and toughen up. Trail runners are rugged where it

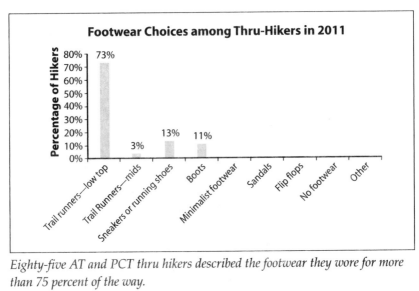

Eighty-five AT and PCT thru hikers described the footwear they wore for more than 75 percent of the way.

counts for backpackers: the toe box and the sole. The rest of the shoe is often made from lightweight materials. With the more rugged and inflexible features of a boot, you'll need to spend a lot of time wearing them to properly break them in, and their intrinsic inflexibility makes them more likely to cause problems with blistering.

Weatherproofing. There's no such thing as a waterproof shoe on a long-distance hike. Don't forget that heavy boots take much longer to dry than a trail runner.

Ankle protection. The biggest myth surrounding the boot is that it provides better ankle support than a low-top trail runner. The fact is, ankle protection comes primarily from the stability of the sole and the heel cup. If your ankles are weak, protect them by purchasing a shoe with a good stiff sole and a deep heel cup that resists excessive side-to-side motion. If you are worried about your ankles, try either hiking with trekking poles or a snug lace-up ankle support. A lace-up support may be a more effective solution than adding the weight of a boot.

The only reason to go with boots is if you expect to encounter mostly snow (in winter hiking), if you'll be doing a significant amount of off-trail travel over sharply uneven terrain like rock, or if you've already got a broken-in old pair hanging around and you want to save money. During the early portions of some trails, such as the AT in Georgia during March, you may be hiking in near-winter conditions and encounter cold temperatures and snow. However, the weather will eventually warm, and you may only need to endure a week or two of nasty weather. Is this worth buying boots? Not in my view. But some choose to do it this way. Three-season trail travel in the United States can be easily done without boots.

Nonetheless, there are successful long-distance hikers who wear boots, and the 2011 surveys identified 9 out of 85 finishers (11 percent) who wore boots most of the way. My wife and I met a hiker in southwest Montana with a heavy pack who was on the tail end of a northbound CDT thru-hike. Along with his big pack, he wore some very sturdy, heavy boots. He was well on his way to finishing the triple crown.

Running shoes are another style of shoe seen on long trails. Sneakers offer no intrinsic protection from the physical obstacles and climate of the trail. They have soles designed for road running, not handling the variable surfaces of trails. Some sneakers have shallower heel cups and thinner soles, meaning less ankle protection.

Running shoes not designed for hiking were also in the footwear minority in the 2011 survey, with just 13 percent making the choice.

Minimalist footwear was inspired by the barefoot running movement and provides little to no structural foot support. This is especially evident in the lack of a raised heel, a ubiquitous feature among running shoes and trail runners alike. If the 2011 survey results are any indication, minimalist footwear does not seem to have caught on among long-distance hikers. None of the 85 thru-hikers reported wearing minimalist footwear for the majority of the trail.

One hiker wrote about his initial footwear choice: "I stupidly thought I could hike in the 'barefoot' type of shoes, but after 200 miles and severe blisters I wisely switched my footwear." While one person's opinion certainly isn't enough reason to rule out the minimalist shoe for long-distance hiking, you do need to consider the lack of shoe structure and the impact of hundreds to thousands of miles on the feet, knees, hips, and spine. It will be interesting to see whether minimalist footwear becomes more accepted among long-distance hikers in years to come.

If you're an experienced hiker and you know you've got really tough feet and ankles, I won't talk you out of wearing sneakers. If this is your first hike, steer away from sneakers until you've put some miles in. If you still want to go with sneakers after you've burned out a pair of trail runners or boots, go for it.

Fit

As feet come in an infinite number of sizes and shapes and shoes come in comparatively fewer, fit can be one of the hardest things to get right. Even when a shoe fits well in the store, there's no guarantee it will fit well on the trail since trail travel adds many more layers of variability to how a shoe fits and performs. Ideally you'd be able to take a shoe out for a week on the trail before you decided to buy it. However, since no outfitter I know of will let you do this, the best you can hope to do is try to mimic trail conditions when trying the shoe on in the store.

If you're serious about your comfort, you may want to get your feet evaluated by a professional before you hit the store. I know this sounds like a departure from the do-it-yourself spirit of this book, but poorly fitting footwear can truly ruin your hike. What you're asking a professional to do is to advise you on the type of shoe that might best support your foot structure. After evaluating your walking style and foot structure, a professional can explain to you what special considerations, if any, to consider when shoe shopping.

There are a few types of professionals who can provide this type of assessment: a podiatrist, a physician with an orthopedic specialty, or a physical therapist with experience in sports injuries or orthopedics. The PT or podiatrist may be more accessible and cost-effective. Be careful about getting this type of assessment from an employee at an outfitter or running store. True, they see lots of feet every day and have experience with shoes, but most don't have the necessary professional training to determine a true foot structure issue and make the right recommendations.

Once you know about style and any special considerations you might have, you'll be ready to go to the outfitter armed with some good information. You and the store associate will be able to narrow down the dozens of shoes on the wall to a few good candidates. Be sure you head to the store with the socks you intend to hike in. If you're going with thick hiker socks and sock liners, that's going to make a difference in how a shoe fits. If you can load up a backpack and bring it along, that's even better. Remember, you're trying your best to predict how footwear will act on the trail. Also, try to get to the store in the afternoon. The volume of the foot can increase by as much as 5 percent during the day, enough to influence shoe sizing.

Before trying a shoe on, take a look at the quality of construction. If you're buying a name-brand shoe from a reputable outfitter, chances are you're getting good quality. All the same, it doesn't hurt to take a look. The different parts of the shoe should adhere together well. Look at the sole of the shoe; does it seem to be firmly attached to the upper part of the shoe? Perform the toe box test by pressing the shoe down at the point where the rubber part of the sole comes up around the front of the toe and attaches to the upper. Does the sole detach from the upper under stress or does it remain firmly attached?

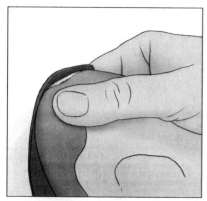

This shoe fails the toe box test.

You should also examine the flexibility of the shoe by performing the torsion test and the flex test. The torsion test is done by grasping the front and back of the shoe and twisting the shoe in opposite directions. The shoe should twist, but you should notice some firmness and resistance as well. This feature is important because you'll be encountering variable terrain on your hike, and you'll need your shoe to be flexible. A completely rigid shoe

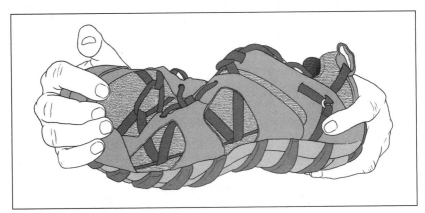

This shoe passes the torsion test.

This shoe fails the torsion test.

that doesn't twist when encountering varied terrain will simply transmit the variability to another part of your foot and ankle, possibly increasing the chances of an ankle injury.

The flex test is completed by once again grasping the front and back of the shoe, but this time pushing the two ends up and together. What you should notice is that the front of the shoe bends and the middle and back of the shoe stay firmly in place. Depending on the thickness of the sole, you may need to put a bit more effort into the test. At a minimum, the front of the shoe should flex about 45 degrees from horizontal as this is the amount of normal motion the toes need to move at the end of a step. Shoes that don't permit this normal amount of toe motion will transmit the motion that doesn't take place in the shoe to another part of the foot, ankle, or even the knee and hip.

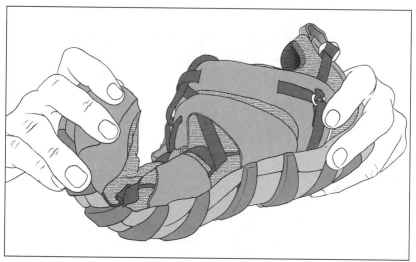

This shoe passes the flex test.

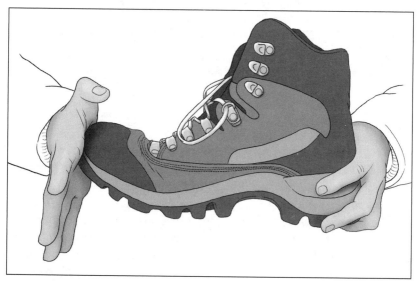

This shoe fails the flex test.

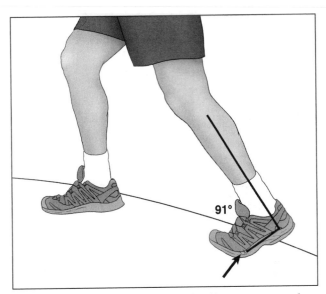

A shoe that passes the flex test will enable a more natural ankle position for heel-off when walking uphill.

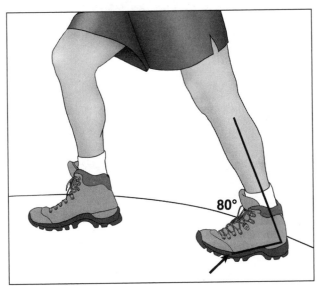

A shoe that fails the flex test will add more strain to the ankle during heel-off when walking uphill.

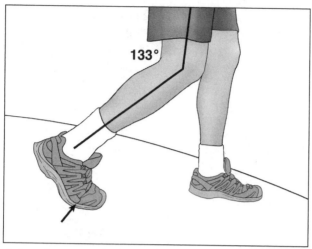

A shoe that passes the flex test will put less strain on the knees when walking downhill.

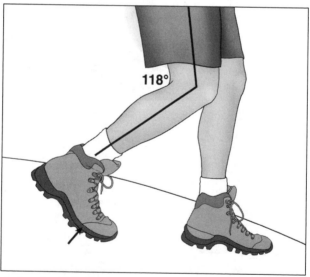

A shoe that fails the flex test will put more strain on the knees when walking downhill.

While doing both tests, keep an eye on the materials of the shoe and take note of any separation of parts. Once you've determined that the shoe is of good quality and flexible, put it on, lace or tighten it up, and walk around. It's best if you're able to put on a loaded backpack while you try your shoes out. If you didn't bring one, see if the store will let you borrow one while you try out your shoes. As you stroll about the store, assess how your feet feel in the shoe. A few things to think about:

- Are you able to walk normally or do you need to make accommodations? Does the shoe feel like it throws you forward or do you have to twist your foot to feel stable? Neither are good features. A good fit allows you to walk like you normally do without accommodations.
- Does your heel feel like it is gripped well by the shoe or does it rub up and down along the back of the shoe? A good-fitting shoe does not piston much at all—your heel doesn't move up and down in it.
- Do your toes feel scrunched? Does the shoe feel too roomy or too tight?
- Does the shoe rub or annoy you anywhere else?
- Does the shoe seem to cradle your feet or does it feel lax and flimsy?

If you notice any issues, take the shoes off and ask for a different size or different model. Be picky and expect to try on several pairs quite possibly from several stores until you get the right fit. Don't be in a hurry to buy.

If the shoe fits well walking around the showroom floor, take it a step further by subjecting the shoe to uneven terrain. You should try to find a vertical incline to do this. Good outfitters will have some sort of artificial hill you can practice on. With your backpack on, go down this hill hard and really try to see if the shoe permits the toes to slide forward and bump into the front of the shoe. If your toes are ramming into the front of the shoe with downhill walking, get a new pair. A little contact with the front of the shoe is OK, but no contact is best. Then try walking up the hill on your toes, keeping note of whether your heel is sliding up and down. A tiny bit of motion is OK, but a good shoe will hold your heel firmly in place. If your outfitter doesn't have a pretend hill, ask to use some stairs or even go outside and find a slope.

If the shoe passes all of the tests, chances are you've got yourself a pair. Congratulations! I hope you didn't pay too much . . .

Stoves

When it comes to picking a stove, you have quite a bit to consider because of the multitude of different stove technologies on the market. These range from simple fuel tablets to sophisticated and complex liquid fuel stoves, all perfectly capable of doing the simple job of heating food and boiling water. The range of choices allows you to chose a stove that fits your style, although there are certain types of stoves that are more suitable than others based on climate and trail location. Deciding which type of stove is right for you involves, like any other gear, weighing a number of factors and deciding on the relative importance of each.

Before delving more thoroughly into the stove decision-making process, the first thing to consider is whether or not you want to carry a stove at all. There are plenty of reasons for going stove-less; weight and volume savings and the ability to eat right away without much setup or clean up are both compelling considerations. If you're the sort of person who values minimizing weight and time taken to complete camp chores above hot food, then the no-stove option might be something to consider.

> Nine percent of finishers in the 2011 thru-hiker survey didn't use a stove.

Be warned, however, that the number of good-tasting, lightweight, high-calorie food options decline precipitously when going stove-less.

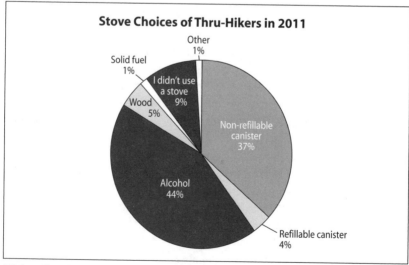

Eighty-five AT and PCT thru-hikers described the stove they carried for more than 75 percent of the way.

Calorie-dense foods like pasta and rice generally require heat and hot water to prepare to the point of palatability. Finding dry food that matches the calorie density of mac and cheese is challenging in a tiny trail town convenience store. This is not to say that the stove-less option is a bad choice. Every year hikers finish long trails with no stoves. It does, however, take a bit more careful attention to food selection and the right temperament.

A final consideration when it comes to choosing stoves is whether or not to make your own. For a first-timer, the idea of homemade gear might sound a little daunting. Stoves, though, are probably the easiest kind of gear to make at home. You can find many designs for free online, and materials are generally inexpensive and readily available at hardware stores. If you have the time and inclination, a homemade stove is a great way to save money. Also, since you'll know exactly how your stove is built, you'll eliminate some of the hassle you might have with a more complex commercial stove. A significant number of thru-hikers chose an alcohol stove, which is the easiest style of stove to make at home.

Essential considerations

If you've decided you want a stove, there are a number of factors to consider that are true with every type of stove. It's up to you to decide how important each of these factors are to your hiking style.

Climate. Do you need a stove that performs well in all kinds of weather conditions?

Fuel availability. Is fuel readily available where you'll be going or do you plan on shipping it to yourself?

Fuel shipping. Will major postal carriers ship the fuel? Will the manufacturer ship it?

Weight. Do you need to minimize weight at all costs? How much does the fuel weigh and how bulky is it?

Cost. Do you have a budget? How much does the fuel cost?

Convenience. Are you content to wait a while or do you need your water boiling as fast as possible? Are you willing to maintain the stove to keep it clean and operational? Do you mind a little setup or takedown? Do you need to be able to modify the intensity of the heat source?

Local regulations. Is your type of stove permitted in the area you're traveling in?

Aesthetics and ecology. Do you care about how your stove looks, smells, or sounds? Do you want to avoid burning petroleum products? Are you trying to minimize waste?

Non-refillable canister stoves

The most common design of a non-refillable (NR) canister stove has a burner with a pot stand attached directly to a metal fuel canister. There are variations of this design, such as the Jetboil, where a cook pot is built directly into the burner. Another variation connects the canister to the burner by a hose.

Climate. NR canister stoves work best in warm climates. Unless the canisters are somehow kept warm, performance in most stove designs declines markedly in below-freezing temperatures. This is because the pressurized gas fuel inside the canister cools to its boiling point and converts to a liquid.

Fuel availability. Fuel for NR canister stoves is typically a mix of butane, isobutane, and propane in pressurized non-refillable metal canisters. Stores in larger trail towns along the AT and PCT will typically sell one or two brands of replacement canisters, but in smaller towns it may be a roll of the dice. In fact, fuel availability, along with weight, were common dislikes among thru-hikers who reported using NR canister stoves in the 2011 survey.

> One hiker writes, "Fuel canisters are more difficult to find in remote resupply locations than bottles of alcohol/HEET. As a result, I often carried 8-ounce canisters instead of 4-ounce canisters since I couldn't count on being able to refuel at my next immediate resupply."

While most burners/canisters from different manufacturers are interchangeable, it's always a good idea to ask about your stove's compatibility with other types of canisters before you buy. Look in a stove's manual for its valve rating. Stoves with an EN417 valve rating will accommodate most canisters.

> NR canister stoves will stop working when the pressurized gas inside the canister becomes a liquid. Gas becomes a liquid when it cools to its boiling point. NR canister stoves are typically filled with a predominant mixture of isobutane or butane, both of which have boiling points higher than what might be experienced on a cold-weather backpacking trip. An NR canister stove using 100 percent isobutane will markedly slow down as temps approach 11 degrees F, which is isobutane's boiling point. If, instead, a stove uses 80 percent isobutane and 20 percent propane, it will stop working at a slightly lower temperature because propane's boiling point is a much colder –44 degrees F. Some NR canister stoves overcome this problem by using a hose to connect the canister to the burner. In very cold weather, when pressurized gas changes to a liquid, the canister can be turned upside down and the stove will continue to receive fuel through gravity flow. This type of assembly adds weight and reduces convenience.

Most fuel must first be converted to a gas in order to light. Flash point is the temperature at which a liquid will give off an ignitable vapor. Liquid fuels like naphtha and gasoline have very low flash points, meaning that if a flame or a spark is lit above them in all but the coldest conditions, the gas will ignite. Denatured alcohol and HEET have flash points in the mid-50s, meaning that in temperatures below these points, stoves using these fuels do not spontaneously ignite with a simple flick of a lighter or match. The fuel must first be preheated. This isn't too difficult to accomplish, and hikers have devised methods to get around the problem of denatured alcohol's high flash point, such as lighting a Vaseline-soaked cotton ball and dropping it into the stove or heating the stove from beneath.

Fuel shipping. NR canister fuels cannot usually be shipped by the U.S. Postal Service because most canister fuels have a flash point below 20 degrees F. See page 48 for the chart on stove fuel properties and pages 49–50 for the chart on U.S. Postal Service shipping regulations.

Weight. The burner is the lightest portion of the stove and some weigh less than two ounces. The canisters, however, make the system a bit heavier, with the smallest canisters available weighing between 6 and 7 ounces when full. Overall, the NR canister stove is in the midrange of weight when compared to other types of stoves.

Cost. NR canister stoves are moderately priced, with ultralight models available for around $60. Fuel economy depends on the size of the canister.

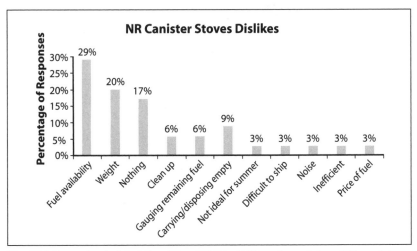

The 31 hikers who finished the AT or PCT in 2011 and carried an NR canister stove provided a total of 35 responses.

Fuel economy is poor with the smallest, lightest canisters. Doubling the size of a canister usually adds little cost, and therefore fuel economy greatly improves with larger canisters. However, carrying larger canisters also adds significant weight.

Convenience. NR canister stoves are one of the more convenient types of stoves. In looking at what 2011 hikers had to say about their NR canister stoves, speed and ease of use seem to be the most appreciated features.

Assembly and takedown is simple, and maintenance for NR canister stoves is almost nil. A hot, intense flame can be had with one flick of a lighter. In many cases, you can easily adjust the intensity of the flame, allowing for a variety of cooking temperatures. Some stoves come equipped with a self-lighting feature, although the reliability of this feature is questionable. When the stove is sheltered from the wind, boil times are the fastest of any type of stove. But these stoves perform poorly in cold temperatures. A small draw-

> One hiker commented about his NR canister stove, "It performed well in all weather conditions. I could throttle the fuel flow for simmering, and it was much more stable than the alcohol stove I started with."

back is not being able to see the quantity of fuel remaining in the canister, though with a little practice, determining remaining fuel becomes easier.

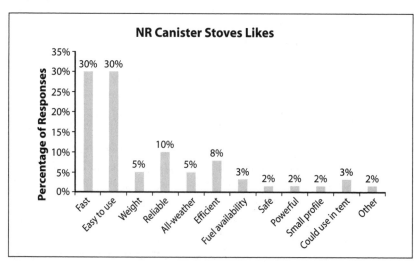

The 31 hikers who finished the AT or PCT in 2011 and carried an NR canister stove provided a total of 63 responses.

Local regulations. NR canister stoves are usually permitted and encouraged in areas where campfires are prohibited. This is because it is easy to control the flame from a canister stove.

Aesthetics and ecology. NR canister stoves are generally whisper-quiet and do not damage or leave films on pots and pans when used correctly. Most fuel canisters cannot be safely refilled and must be disposed of when emptied. As canisters are made of steel or aluminum, they could potentially be recycled in localities that are able to handle these materials, although some may require that the canister first be punctured and completely emptied. If proper disposal and recycling is important to you on a long-distance hike, consider how practical this might be in a small trail town. Check your own locality's recycling rules for further clarification. Canisters use petroleum-based fuel.

Overall thoughts. If boiling water quickly, efficiently, and without much hassle is important to you and you don't mind spending a little money up front, then the NR canister stove is a good choice. If you're spending a lot of time in cold weather, traveling far from outdoors-oriented towns, or have strong ecological sensibilities, then you might want to try another stove model.

Alcohol stoves

The alcohol stove's simple design departs substantially from the more complex design of canister stoves. While a few models are available commercially, many alcohol stoves seen on long trails are homemade, owing to the ease by which they can be built. Instructions for building an alcohol stove can be found online.

Alcohol stoves come in all different shapes and forms, but the basic design involves a metal receptacle into which fuel is poured and lit to create a flame. A pot can be suspended over the flame by means of a pot stand. Pot stands are also easy to build and can often be incorporated into a homemade windscreen for a

> A good place to find instructions on how to make your own alcohol stove is http://zenstoves.net/Construction.htm.

very light and compact stove assembly. Some models have a double wall and burner holes to create a more steady, even flame.

Climate. Like NR canister stoves, alcohol stoves are easiest to operate in warmer climates. This is because fuel for alcohol stoves is typically denatured alcohol or a more widely available product called HEET, both of which have flash points in the mid-50s. Because alcohol stoves also have a

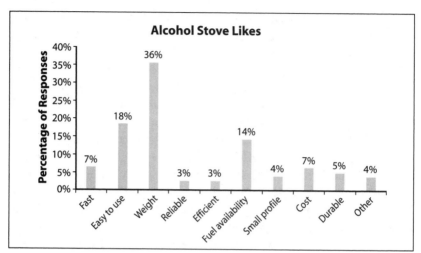

The 39 hikers who finished the AT or PCT in 2011 and carried an alcohol stove provided a total of 76 responses.

weaker flame, they are also more susceptible to the wind and should be used behind a good windbreak in order to function optimally.

Fuel availability. Fuel for alcohol stoves is widely available, adding to its appeal. Denatured alcohol can be found in hardware stores with the paint thinners. Stores in trail towns along the popular AT and PCT often stock denatured alcohol as they are used to distance hikers asking for it. HEET, normally used as a gas line anti-freeze and water remover in vehicles, can be found in most gas station convenience stores. HEET in the yellow bottle (methyl alcohol) is a better stove fuel than HEET in the red bottle (isopropyl alcohol).

Fuel shipping. Denatured alcohol and HEET can both be shipped with appropriate packing and labeling, giving alcohol stoves a notable advantage in this category over unshippable NR canister fuel.

Weight. Survey results from AT and PCT thru-hikers confirm that when it comes to what they like best about alcohol stoves, weight is overwhelmingly popular. Alcohol stoves are often touted as being the lightest of all stoves. This is a half-truth. Indeed, the stoves themselves are extremely light. Homemade versions made from soda or cat food cans weigh less than half an ounce, and commercially sold alcohol stoves with a few more bells and whistles weigh a tad more than an ounce. What should not be

Water weighs 8.3 pounds per gallon (1kg/L).

overlooked, however, is the weight of the fuel. Weighing just 20 percent less than water, denatured alcohol and HEET are two of the heaviest liquid fuels that can be used with backpacking stoves. Nonetheless, the alcohol stove still has a distinct weight advantage over most of its peers on a long-distance hike. This is because the wide availability of denatured alcohol in small towns permits transport of the fuel in smaller amounts.

Cost. The alcohol stove is among the lowest cost stoves, especially if it is homemade. Fuel is inexpensive and fuel economy is good, although costs can increase substantially if care is not taken to shield and protect the flame for optimal efficiency.

Convenience. Alcohol stoves, due to their simple designs, don't take long to set up. For designs featuring an open fuel reservoir, simply pour fuel in and light to get a flame. Users of alcohol stoves must take more care to shield their cooking assembly in windy conditions as alcohol stoves have a much less intense flame than canister stoves. Lower flame intensity means that alcohol stoves also tend to have slower boiling times than canister stoves. Alcohol stoves require zero maintenance, unless you use fuel that burns dirty and clogs the vents. Fuel for alcohol stoves requires pre-heating in temps below the mid to lower 50s. Alcohol stoves burn only the amount of fuel that is placed in the reservoir. If fuel runs out and additional

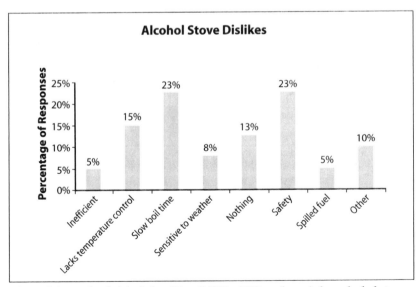

The 39 hikers who finished the AT or PCT in 2011 and carried an alcohol stove provided a total of 40 responses.

burn time is needed, the stove must be refilled and relit, adding to boil time. Adding additional fuel to the stove while it is lit is extremely dangerous. You usually can't modify the intensity of the flame or simmer foods on simple alcohol stoves unless you are carrying a simmering attachment, which can be cumbersome to use.

Finally, because many take advantage of minimalist design, alcohol stoves can be trickier to handle than more conventional stoves. Thru-hikers using alcohol stoves in 2011 reported the sometimes unpredictable nature and lack of features in the alcohol stove as common complaints. More than any other stove type, hikers using alcohol stoves reported difficulty controlling the flame, leading to occasional melted windscreens and singed hairs.

Local regulations. Because you can't control the flame as well as with other stoves and you can accidentally spill the fuel, alcohol stoves may not be permitted in areas where fire danger is high or where campfires are prohibited.

Aesthetics and ecology. Some consider alcohol stoves more aesthetically pleasing—they are completely silent and have a fairly small footprint, and some people like using homemade gear. Alcohol stoves are not completely odorless, although this depends on fuel type. Ecologically speaking, denatured alcohol comes from various mixtures of renewable and nonrenewable resources, depending on the manufacturer.

Overall thoughts. The alcohol stove is a favorite of thru-hikers due to its low cost, convenience, and weight. If these features are important to

---

Authorities managing public lands in very dry or otherwise delicate regions often enact campfire bans. In some places, alcohol and wood burning stoves, though not technically campfires, may still be banned or restricted because you can't control the fire as well as you can with other types of stoves. It's important to get the restrictions for your stove clarified if you are traveling in an area with a fire ban.

Over the years, authorities managing public lands along the AT and PCT have grown accustomed to seeing long-distance hikers carrying homemade alcohol stoves, and as we are generally considered a responsible group, alcohol stoves have been permitted in most places. If you are not sure your alcohol stove is permitted in a fire ban, make sure you ask.

Woodstoves are less familiar to authorities and, though they are easier to control than alcohol stoves, more closely resemble a campfire and are less likely to be permitted. Nonetheless, rangers and other park authorities can be persuaded to allow a wood-burning stove if you present yourself as a responsible and experienced user. Again, make sure you seek permission or an exception first rather than waiting to be caught. It's important that all long-distance hikers act responsibly so that we can continue using the stoves we like.

you and you don't mind longer boiling times, can learn to responsibly manage a flame that can sometimes be challenging to control, and are able to adapt in windy or cold conditions, then the alcohol stove is a good choice, especially when you have short distances between resupply points and can carry smaller amounts of fuel at a time.

Refillable canister stoves

Refillable canister stoves, like NR canister stoves, feature a burner assembly and a fuel canister. With a refillable stove, however, the burner is attached to the fuel canister from a distance by a hose rather than mounted flush to the canister by a threaded screw. Canisters are equipped with pumps, which move the liquid fuel to the burner, where it is heated, vaporized, and burned. They hold liquid fuel instead of pressurized gas.

Climate. Refillable canister stoves are notably better cold-weather performers than NR canister stoves because they do not rely on the intrinsic pressure of gas. They also perform better in cold weather than most alcohol stoves because they can accommodate fuels with a range of flash and boiling points.

Fuel availability. Although some brands prefer you only use a certain type of fuel, an advantage of the refillable model over the NR canister model is the ability to refill the canister with any kind of liquid fuel. Naphtha, kerosene, gasoline, or even jet fuel will work with these stoves, potentially increasing the likelihood that you'll be able to refill in trail towns.

Fuel shipping. Shipping fuel for use in a refillable canister stove depends on the flash point of the fuel. Recall that a fuel's flash point is the temperature at which the fuel will produce an ignitable vapor. Naphtha (aka white gas, Coleman fuel) is a commonly used fuel in refillable canister stoves and cannot be shipped by the U.S. Postal Service due to its low flash point. Fuels with high flash points, like jet fuel A and kerosene, can be shipped. See page 48 for the chart on stove fuel properties and pages 49–50 for the chart on U.S. Postal Service shipping regulations.

Weight. Due to hoses and other parts, burners for refillable canister stoves weigh more and take up more space than burners for NR canister stoves. Lightweight models weigh between 8 and 9 ounces. Weight of the refillable canisters vary according to capacity and, to a much lesser extent, the type of fuel carried. Because of their additional bulk, refillable canisters are the heaviest of their peers. Indeed, weight was the complaint from two of the three thru-hikers who carried this type of stove and took the survey in 2011.

Responses to "What did you like the least about your stove?"

- Weight.
- Taking off the pressurized canister, always got a little bit of gas on my hands.
- The weight in combination with the fuel and pot.

Cost. A good, lightweight model will cost about $100 with an extra $15 for the canister. Fuel is inexpensive, and fuel economy is excellent. The refillable canister stove is one of the least expensive stoves to operate. However, it will take many nights out for this stove's good fuel economy to be worth its high initial price tag. Heavier models can be had for less money. It's important to also note that certain liquid fuels may be hard to find in small trail towns, and shipping fuel up the trail will increase its cost and therefore decrease fuel economy.

Convenience. Of all stove types, refillable canister stoves require the most maintenance due to their small O-rings, hoses, and pumps. They also require pumping and priming to move liquid fuel to the burner and heat the fuel enough to vaporize it so it can become a flame. I have seen more people struggle with operating refillable canister stoves than any other type. However, when regularly cleaned and maintained, refillable canister stoves become much more reliable to use. Maintenance kits are sold for refillable canister stoves. Otherwise, the refillable canister stove has many of the same convenient features of a non-refillable canister stove, including the ability to modify the flame intensity and a hot, intense flame for fast boil times. It is worth noting that certain liquid fuels burn dirtier than others and will affect how often the stove needs to be cleaned.

Local regulations. Refillable canister stoves are usually permitted and encouraged in areas where campfires are prohibited. This is because you can control the flame from a canister stove.

Aesthetics and ecology. Refillable canister stoves are louder than non-refillable canister stoves and make a whooshing sound when in operation. Some fuels, such as diesel and kerosene, smell bad and smoke quite a bit, quickly clogging the stove. The poor aesthetics of refillable canister stoves are partially made up for by the ecological benefits of being able to refill the canisters.

Overall thoughts. Refillable canister stoves are recommended if rapid boiling time is important and you don't mind performing regular cleaning and maintenance as well as being observant to detail when lighting the stove, as refillable canister stoves take a bit more work to get a steady flame going. They are superior to non-refillable canister stoves in cold weather. If aesthetics, low maintenance, no-hassle setup, and ultralight travel are more important, you might want to consider a different model of stove.

Woodstoves

Woodstoves are far less common, but often just as viable an option as canister and alcohol stoves for long-distance hiking trips. Woodstoves typically feature a central, ventilated chamber for burning tiny, finger-sized chips of wood. Some are equipped with battery-powered fans to provide air flow to the fire; others create air flow through creative stove design features. There are a multitude of designs made today, most by small craftspeople. It's rare to encounter a woodstove taking up shelf space at a large outdoor retailer.

> Woodstoves that don't have a fan rely on the chimney effect to provide natural air flow through the stove: when hot gas from the flame rises, vents placed below the flame cause air to be sucked into the stove.

Climate. Woodstoves work in all climates where there is a supply of wood scraps. Similar to alcohol stoves, woodstoves have a weaker flame than canisters and can perform poorly in windy conditions. Woodstoves also may not work as well in wet conditions where dry wood is harder to find.

Fuel availability. The great advantage of a woodstove is not needing to carry or ration fuel. This makes a woodstove extremely portable and usable nearly anywhere in the world where wood can be found. The flipside is that in rainy conditions, where dry wood is difficult to find, starting and maintaining a hot fire will be labor-intensive. Proponents of woodstoves often carry extra dry tinder for wet days as well as reliable fire-starting materials. Expert users claim that even in wet conditions you can usually find dry wood.

Fuel shipping. The cost and hassle associated with shipping fuel for other stove technologies is negligible since fuel for a wood stove is gathered on the trail.

Weight. Considering that you need to carry fuel for both alcohol and canister stoves, woodstoves are competitive in the weight category, although they are not the lightest. The Bushbuddy Ultra model of woodstove, for example, weighs 6.6 ounces. What's nice about the woodstove is that its weight is stable. Other types of stoves can be fairly heavy at the start of a trip, only becoming lighter as you use the fuel.

Cost. A considerable amount of work goes into building a lightweight, high-quality woodstove, so prices tend to run high for ultralight models ($115 to $150). Heavier models cost half the price. Woodstoves can be built at home, saving in cost, but building a good quality woodstove is much more complicated than building an alcohol stove.

On a positive financial note, fuel is free, and a good quality woodstove will last a long time. However, a woodstove would have to be used for a fairly long time to make up for its high initial cost when compared to less expensive stoves like those that burn alcohol. In the 2011 survey, the four hikers who used woodstoves pointed to the availability of free fuel as what they liked the most.

Responses to "What did you like the most about your stove?"

- Lightweight.
- The fact that I could cook and have hot drinks all the times I wished.
- No fuel cost and one less item we had to worry about in town.
- Not having to worry about fuel.

Dislikes were a little more varied:

- Fiddling with it at the end of the day.
- In windy spots is hard to manage.
- Prep time.
- It took too long, and the Ti-Tri and case took up too much space. We switched to our Pocket Rocket in Washington. I would use that the whole way on another hike.

Convenience. The convenience of using a woodstove varies considerably with climate and stove design. You can make a hot fire quickly in dry, still conditions where wood is easy to find. In wet climates or during periods of rain, woodstoves can be painstakingly difficult to operate, and meticulous care must be taken to find dry wood. Woodstoves that feature an open top for holding a pot need a secure windbreak. Those that do not feature an open top will be less vulnerable to the wind, but many of these models only boil water and do not accommodate a pot. A side benefit of carrying a woodstove is that your fire-starting skills markedly improve. Nonetheless, in cold, windy, wet weather, some woodstoves may be practically unusable to even the most skilled fire starter. In consolation, a woodstove, once burning, provides an unlimited source of heat to warm its user. Canister stoves and alcohol stoves are often switched off after use to conserve fuel and don't provide the same kind of cheer and warmth that can be had from a wood fire.

Local regulations. Woodstoves may be prohibited where campfire bans are in effect.

Aesthetics and ecology. Woodstoves get good marks for aesthetics and ecology, although those equipped with a fan make noise and require batteries. In the outdoors, wood fires are about as natural a form of fuel as possible. Woodstoves also work best with dead or downed materials that are native to where you are traveling; no carting in petroleum-based fuel. One aesthetic/ecological complaint that can be lodged against the woodstove is that, depending on the type and moisture level of wood used, it can produce a copious amount of smoke. Woodstoves also blacken the bottom of cook pots with creosote and care must be taken to keep the cook pot separate from other items in the pack. Woodstoves with battery-operated fans also make noise, though woodstoves without fans are silent save the crackling and popping of wood.

> Woodstoves are my favorite stove. I used one through the northern half of the PCT and along the Montana section of the CDT. But I have found woodstoves to be sometimes difficult to use in wet climates like northern New England.

Overall thoughts. If you value a more natural backcountry experience, enjoy a wood fire, and don't mind waiting for hot water, accepting that in some conditions getting a hot fire going may be a painfully slow or impossible process, then this is your stove. If a quick, no-hassle cooking experience is your priority, you may want to consider another stove type.

Solid fuel

There's really more to say about the fuel than the actual stove when it comes to solid fuel. This is because you can burn solid fuel in just about any type of stove. Many stoves designed to burn wood or denatured alcohol can just as easily burn solid fuel. In fact, all that's needed for a basic solid fuel stove is material to protect the stove from the ground and a pot stand.

> Of the 85 thru-hikers responding to the 2011 survey, only 1 reported using solid fuel. She liked that solid fuel was lightweight, but found that it didn't get her water "super hot."

Climate. Of all stove types, solid fuel is perhaps the most versatile when it comes to climate. The only drawback is that, like wood and alcohol stoves, the solid fuel flame is susceptible to being blown around in the wind, so a windbreak is important.

The Physical Properties of Common Stove Fuels

Fuel	Flash Point (°F)	Boiling Point (°F)	Relative Density (water = 1.0)
Butane	−76	31.1	0.58 (gas)
Denatured alcohol	45–55	173	0.81
Diesel fuel (No.2)	140–176	356–644	0.85
ESBIT (hexamine)	482	536	1.3
Gasoline	−45	80–437	6.0–6.5
HEET (yellow bottle)	52	148	0.80
Isobutane	−115	11	0.56 (gas)
Jet fuel A	101–162	350–550	0.80
Kerosene	100	300–617	0.76–0.84
Naphtha (Coleman fuel, white gas)	0	320–430	0.70
Propane	−156	−44	0.42 (gas)

Fuel availability. The more commonly known solid fuel is the ESBIT tab. ESBIT tabs are widely available online and at outfitters. However, don't count on finding them in all small trail towns. A long-distance hiker relying on ESBIT will likely have to ship the tabs via mail drops.

Fuel shipping. ESBIT is classified by the USPS as a "flammable solid" and may be shipped in amounts less than 1 pound if labeled appropriately.

Weight. Using ESBIT fuel with a minimalist stove design is one of the lightest ways to travel.

Cost. Costing roughly $0.50 to boil two cups of water, ESBIT has one of the worst fuel economies of any fuel. ESBIT becomes even more expensive if it has to be shipped to mail drops. However, because an ESBIT stove can be made for a fraction of the cost of a canister stove or woodstove, the overall cost of an ESBIT stove remains low for all but the longest trips.

Convenience. The ease of portability and ignition make solid fuel stoves one of the most convenient types of stoves available. They don't have any of the maintenance requirements of refillable canister stoves and don't have cold-weather issues like non-refillable canister and alcohol stoves. Conversely, solid fuel stoves tend to lack frills like the ability to simmer and modify flame intensity, though if you're clever with engineering, you can design a stove structure for solid fuel to fit your exact needs.

U.S. Postal Service Shipping Regulations

Source: USPS Publication 52, Hazardous Materials Table, Postal Service Mailability Guide

Fuel	Shippable by USPS?	Notes/Instructions
Butane	No	Flash Point <20°F
Denatured alcohol	Yes	3A
Diesel fuel (No.2)	Yes	3A-1
ESBIT (hexamine)	Yes	4A
Gasoline	No	Flash Point <20°F
HEET (yellow bottle)	Yes	3A
Isobutane	No	Flash Point <20°F
Jet fuel A	Yes	3A-1
Kerosene	Yes	3A-1
Naphtha (Coleman fuel, white gas)	No	Flash Point <20°F
Propane	No	Flash Point <20°F

	3A	3A-1
Primary Receptacle (container that the fuel is in)	A metal primary receptacle must not exceed 1 quart.	A metal primary receptacle must not exceed 1 gallon.
	A nonmetal primary receptacle must not exceed 1 pint.	A nonmetal primary receptacle must not exceed 1 quart.
	The primary receptacle must have a screw cap (with minimum of one-and-one-half turns), soldering clips, or other means of secure closure (friction tops are not acceptable).	
	Only one primary receptacle is permitted per mail piece.	
Cushioning Material and Secondary Packaging	Enough cushioning material must surround the primary receptacle to prevent breakage and absorb any potential leakage.	
	The cushioning and primary receptacle must be packed in securely sealed secondary packaging.	
Outer Packaging	Strong outer packaging that is capable of firmly and securely holding the primary receptacle, cushioning material, and secondary packaging is required.	
Marking	Each mail piece must be clearly marked on the address side with "Surface Only" or "Surface Mail Only" and "Consumer Commodity ORM–D."	
	A complete return address and delivery address must be used.	

	4A
Primary Receptacle (container that the fuel is in)	The primary receptacle must have a secure seal and together with its contents must not exceed a weight of 1 pound.
	Multiple primary receptacles are permitted.

(continued on page 50)

(continued from page 49)	4A
Cushioning Material and Secondary Packaging	Sufficient cushioning material must be used to absorb shock and protect the primary receptacle from breakage.
Outer Packaging	Strong outer packaging that is capable of firmly and securely holding the primary receptacle and cushioning material is required.
	Each mail piece must not exceed a total weight of 25 pounds.
Marking	Each mail piece must be clearly marked on the address side with "Surface Only" or "Surface Mail Only" and "Consumer Commodity ORM–D."
	A complete return address and delivery address must be used.

Local regulations. Solid fuel may be prohibited where campfire bans are in effect.

Aesthetics and ecology. Some people find the odor produced by burning solid fuel to be objectionable. ESBIT is mostly hexamine, a chemical made from the reaction of ammonia and formaldehyde. It may not, therefore, appeal to those with strong ecological views. Solid fuel will also cover cook pots with residue, so take care to keep cook pots separate from other items in the pack.

Overall thoughts. If you don't mind chemical smells or scum on the bottom of your pot, and don't wish to make an upfront investment in a more complex stove technology, consider using solid fuel, especially if you'll be experiencing a wide range of climates and value light and fast travel.

Water Treatment

On overnight hikes of any length, I have always carried along some sort of means for sanitizing water. My method has evolved over the years, based on personal preferences and priorities. For the majority of the AT, I carried a pump filter. While the pump filter consistently delivered clean, clear water, I eventually grew tired of the routines and maintenance associated with pumping and craved greater simplicity and a lighter pack. So for the first half of the PCT, I used iodine crystals, which satisfied my need for a fast and hassle-free way of making my water safe. However, I didn't like the way that iodine discolored my water bottle, and I started to dislike it's subtle, but noticeable taste. Iodine was especially disappointing in pristine areas like the Sierra Nevada, where I most wanted to drink water without iodine tinge. For the second half of the PCT, I switched back to filtration, this time using a gravity filter. For me, this was essentially a way to get the hassle-free nature of chemicals, but without the chemical taste. Today my choice continues to be either the gravity filter or ultraviolet light, depending on where I'm going and whether I'm traveling solo or with a partner.

Water treatment technology exists to make backcountry water potable by either deactivating harmful organisms or filtering them out. Waterborne organisms found in backcountry water can be grouped into three main classes: protozoa, bacteria, and viruses. I won't go into great detail on the subject of water microbiology, but it's helpful to understand some basics. Protozoans are a type of single-celled organism and tend to be the largest of the three classes. Some are capable of self-propulsion, and many parasitic protozoans are able to form cysts, allowing them to survive outside their host in harsh environments. In the United States and Canada, the most well-known protozoan in water that causes sickness is *Giardia lamblia*. This small, flagellated organism attaches itself to the intestinal linings of its host before morphing into a tiny cyst and floating down the digestive tract to be passed as stool. *Giardia* affects it host by preventing nutrients from being absorbed in the intestine. *Cryptosporidium* is another notorious protozoan.

Bacteria are also single-celled organisms, but they lack the internal cellular structures of protozoans and are usually smaller in size. Protozoans often feed on bacteria. The more well-known waterborne bacteria in the wilderness include *E. coli* and *Salmonella*. Bacteria are transmitted through contaminated animal and human feces, either through direct contact, drinking contaminated water, or eating contaminated food.

Viruses are the tiniest of the three—so small that they're capable of evading most backpacking filters. A virus invades a host cell and uses the host's own architecture to replicate. The viruses most commonly associated with wilderness water contamination in the United States and Canada are collectively known as noroviruses. The term "norovirus," or Norwalk-like virus, describes a number of distinct viruses with similar characteristics. They are spread to humans by contact with human feces or vomit or by close contact with an infected person. While human noroviruses have traditionally been thought to be transmitted only by human-to-human contact, a recent body of evidence suggests that human noroviruses might also be transmitted through contact with cow and pig feces, although no definitive conclusions have yet to be drawn.

With three different kinds of organisms to be concerned with, it stands to reason that carrying along a method to make water potable is a sensible thing to do. However, it isn't so straightforward.

Among any random group of long-distance hikers, you inevitably find a small minority of folks who decline to carry any type of water treatment. They can be seen out on the trail scooping up water on the go and drinking it down with abandon. Since widely accepted wilderness mantra dictates that no backcountry water is safe to drink untreated, this might seem like lunacy to most of us, but do the non-treaters have a point?

The decision whether to carry water treatment, just like with any type of backpacking gear, depends on an individual's assessment of risk weighed against the loss of convenience and contribution to pack weight associated with using and transporting a method for treating water. To make such an assessment, it would be helpful to quantify one's risk of getting sick from drinking untreated

Sure enough, a surprising 16½ percent of thru-hikers who finished and filled out the 2011 survey didn't normally treat their water.

backcountry water, an event that usually results in diarrhea, stomach pain, dehydration, and significant time off the trail. Unfortunately, to date, there isn't any scientific research that definitively quantifies this risk. Such research would be practically impossible to undertake, owing to the fact that different backcountry areas have different land-usage patterns. A 2008 study out of the University of California and the California Department of Public Health examined the presence of coliform bacteria along different portions of the Sierra Nevada in California. Checking for coliform bacteria is a way of tracking risk for waterborne pathogens because its presence is indicative of fecal contamination in waterways. The authors of the study sampled Sierran wilderness water over five years from areas with the following patterns of use:

1. Not visited by humans or domesticated animals
2. Visited only by day hikers where overnight camping was prohibited
3. Visited by overnight backpackers, but pack stock prohibited
4. Traversed by pack stock (horses and mules)
5. Cattle- and sheep-grazing tracts

What the researchers found was that the percentage of samples containing coliform bacteria varied based on land use:

1. No humans or domestic animals: 9 percent
2. Day hikers: 12 percent
3. Overnight backpacking sites, no pack stock: 18 percent

4. Pack stock areas: 63 percent
5. Cattle- and sheep-grazing tracts: 96 percent

The presence of coliform bacteria did not vary by elevation or temperature.

The study shows that wilderness areas where pack stock and sheep and cattle grazing are permitted have the greatest fecal contamination. Since fecal contamination introduces organisms causing waterborne illnesses into waterways, it stands to reason that drinking water from areas where domestic animal grazing and pack stock are permitted place backpackers at greater risk for contracting a waterborne illness. Other areas, such as overnight backpacker and day hiker sites where pack stock is not permitted can be expected to contain far less fecal contamination. Knowing that not all contaminated water contains organisms that can cause sickness, the individual long-distance hiker, if drinking water only from these areas, needs to decide for himself how to handle risk of not treating water. Some considerations:

- Along most of the Continental Divide and Pacific Crest Trails, long-distance hikers do not camp in designated areas. However, the PCT and CDT often pass through or close to lands where domestic grazing is permitted. Also notable is that pack stock are permitted along the entire length of the PCT and CDT.
- Along the more populous AT, long-distance hikers often camp in more high-use places like shelters, often with designated places (privies) to defecate, although not everyone chooses to do so. Pack stock are not permitted on the AT, although cattle grazing is present in certain areas.

My own take on packing along a method for water treatment is pragmatic. Since treating water is a fairly easy thing to do and many methods don't make an excessive contribution to pack weight and volume, it's easier for me to carry a water treatment method than to worry endlessly about water sources. Unless you are traveling consistently above tree line, it is often difficult to ascertain what land-use patterns are upstream. On the other hand, deciding to not pack along a method for treating water is not a completely unreasonable decision for those who are comfortable with a higher level of risk. Non-treaters should follow a well-disciplined approach to keep their risk as low as possible:

- When drinking trailside water, take from the upstream portion of the trail, well away from any signs of hoofprints.

- Try to source water in places where nearby land-use patterns can be assessed. Don't source water if you know grazing is taking place upstream.
- Avoid sourcing water from large, more static bodies of water like lakes and ponds, which may be fed by a number of possible contaminated sources and are likely to be a habitat for animals like beavers, who can carry waterborne pathogens in their stool.
- Along the AT, water taken from a shelter source should be used only for cooking and should be boiled, since not everyone uses the privies or deposits stool the recommended 100 feet from water sources. This is especially true along the more high-use portions like the Great Smoky Mountains National Park.

Those choosing to forgo water treatment along the CDT and PCT will have a tough time outside of pristine areas like the High Sierra Nevada or Glacier National Park, since sometimes the only water sources available for many, many miles are heavily cattle contaminated. A hybrid approach, where you carry water treatment for the contaminated sections, might work but will add to logistical complexity.

Essential considerations

My good friend Optimist once called me to talk about treating water. He and his wife Stopwatch had hiked a stretch of the PCT with me in 2007, and they were getting ready to attempt a thru-hike of the AT. I had just finished researching and writing an article for an online publication on gravity filters and ultraviolet (UV) light, so I was ready to talk shop. Our conversation carried on with Optimist doing most of the talking. I asked him what they thought was the most important thing they valued in getting water ready for drinking. Did they need water to be ready instantaneously with no extra work? Did they prioritize taste or were they happy with a little trace of chemical flavor? Were they worried about the health risks of using iodine over the long term? Did they mind carrying batteries? I knew that they had used chlorine bleach on the PCT, so I had a sense of what they were looking for. Since they valued convenience above everything else, the decision came down to UV light or chemical filtration. They wanted to save money; the chemicals were light, cheap, and work fast; and they were traveling as a couple, so Optimist and Stopwatch again chose chlorine bleach.

If you've decided to carry a method for treating water, like Optimist and Stopwatch, then it's time to decide which method to choose. Just like advances in stoves, the technologies available for treating water are highly diverse and often technologically complex, but they can essentially be broken down into four main categories: filtration, chemicals, UV light, and boiling. While bringing water to a rolling boil for a full minute (adding an extra minute per 1,000 feet above sea level) is by far the most reliable way to kill all waterborne pathogens, it's time- and fuel-consuming and therefore impractical for long-distance hiking. So what follows are considerations for choosing filters, chemicals, or UV light.

What's important to keep in mind when choosing a water treatment technology is that there is no such thing as a perfect system, that is, a system that is ultralight; convenient for all terrain; delivers clean, taste-free water; is low maintenance and inexpensive; and filters all three types of waterborne pathogens. You might hear experts talk about how one type of water treatment system is better than another based on all of the things it can kill, filter out, or render sterile, but this is only one consideration. For a light and fast hiker, the absolute number of waterborne pathogens treated might be less of a consideration if the technology adds weight and time. Others are willing to carry a few extra ounces and do a bit more work for clean-tasting, pathogen-free water. So while you're reading ahead, keep in mind that each kind of system has its own unique characteristics and drawbacks and consider them in light of your own hiking style. The total number of waterborne pathogens treated may be the most important thing for you, or it might not. It's up to you to decide what's important and weigh the benefits and drawbacks.

Probably the first thing to consider when deciding on a technology is whether or not coverage for viruses is necessary, since opting for virus coverage will simplify your options. Viruses, owing to their very small size, cannot be removed by most backpacking filters. The pores of most filters come about as small as 0.1 micrometers (microns). Viruses, many falling somewhere between 20 and 40 nanometers, are considerably smaller. So if you're thinking about virus coverage, most filters are out. There are a few exceptions, but these filters either incorporate chemical technology or are so heavy and slow flowing as to be prohibitive for long-distance hiking.

Once again, you need to consider the risk. Viruses are mainly spread from human to human. Thus, for a human virus to be consumed in drinking water, that water would need to be contaminated by human waste. This would seem to rule out cattle- and pack stock–contaminated water as a source of human virus, although recent research shows that this assumption may not technically be true. If you're the type of person who can set this type of technicality aside and are comfortable with the idea that viral contamination in water is rare in the backcountry, then you may reasonably chose to forgo virus coverage in your water treatment. If, however, you are planning on traveling downstream of large to medium-sized human population centers, you might elect to carry virus protection owing to the increasing likelihood of encountering water contaminated by human feces and, by extension, viruses.

Personally, I don't feel I need virus coverage and am comfortable with the relatively low risk of contracting a waterborne virus in comparison to bacteria and protozoa. I mainly hike upstream from major population centers and on the trail try to source water upstream, where human contamination is less likely. If you are traveling outside the United States and Canada to a place where human viral contamination is more likely or unknown, opt for viral coverage.

Before reading about how each kind of technology breaks down, understand that treating water is only one of two essential steps in preventing digestive illnesses on the trail. Hikers who exercise poor hygiene and fail to clean their hands after pooping become a potential vector for all three classes of waterborne pathogen. It's good practice to carry a tiny bottle of alcohol-based hand cleanser and to use it immediately after every bowel movement. Ask anyone who has come down with a digestive illness on the trail: 1 ounce of this stuff is a negligible price to pay considering the agonizing cost of being sick.

Filtration

There are lots of good reasons to use filters for treating water. Water treated by a filter doesn't have a chemical taste and you don't need to use batteries, so the device works as long as the filter stays reasonably clean. That said, there are also a good many reasons not to use a filter. So if you're thinking about using filters, you've got a little more technology to learn about. Filtration technology breaks down into three additional subcategories: pump, gravity, and inline. While they all have filtration in common, the methods by which these technologies achieve filtration are diverse and cater to a wide range of styles.

Before diving in, here's a quick primer on what filtration actually is. Filters essentially strain out waterborne pathogens by physically blocking them. Any organism or solid that is larger than the pores of the filter stays out of the drinking water. Most high-quality backpacking filters have pore sizes of 0.1 to 0.2 micrometers (microns), thus keeping all harmful protozoans and bacteria out of the drinking water because these organisms won't fit through the pores. Filters also trap suspended solids like silt. With a few exceptions, viruses will pass through filters because they are smaller than the pores of filters. What separates most filter technologies is the means by which water is forced through the filter. With a pump filter, you use a hand pump. You hang a gravity filter, and water moves through the filter passively. You attach inline filters to the end of your bottle and drink directly from it, using mouth suction and squeezing. Here is how they stack up against each other.

Pump filters

Pump filters are perhaps the most widely known form of water treatment. Whether this is because they're older technology or because the big box outdoor retailers tend to feature them more prominently than other types of water treatments (in some stores, pump filters and a few selections of chemicals are the only choices) is up for debate. In any event, I think there are very few reasons to go with a pump filter for long-distance hiking.

Setup and maintenance. Of all technologies for water treatment, pump filters require the most setup and maintenance. You usually need to attach an input and output line, watch out for a moving pump handle, and periodically clean the filter. Anyone who has seen vegetation growing on the inside of his hoses will tell you that these should periodically be cleaned as well.

> Hikers in the 2011 survey who used pump filters often reported that the devices were heavy and that pumping became difficult once the filters started to clog.

Convenience. Water is pumped through the device by hand, which can be a tedious process if the filter is in need of cleaning. Unless you scoop untreated water into another container and bring it to camp, pump filters essentially require you to squat at water's edge and pump away, filling up the water bottle one squirt at a time. This is a harmless, pleasant task on a warm sunny day, but in a slightly-above-freezing drizzle or a downpour this process can be total misery, no matter how fast the flow rate of the device (the rate at which water is moved through the filter). On the positive side, pump filters allow you to make as much or as little water as you need at one time, which can be convenient if the distance between reliable water sources is small. Also, input hoses on pump filters can suck up water directly from shallow pools, a task that is much more difficult with any other technology.

Weight. Ounce for ounce, pump filters outweigh most other forms of water treatment. The lightest come in at 8 ounces and the heaviest are over a pound. Average weights are somewhere around 11 to 12 ounces.

Price. The total cost to treat 500 quarts of water on the trail with a pump filter is anywhere from $80 to $115. One high-end model has a purchase price of $370, but that's impractical for most long-distance hikers. If a filter is well maintained and water treated is not excessively mucky, most hikers can go several thousand miles before needing to change filters. An additional cost consideration is that the plastic housing of most pump filters makes them susceptible to breaking when dropped.

Taste. Unaltered.

Time to potability. A big advantage for the pump filter over chemicals is that water can be consumed as quickly as it can be moved through the pump. There's no wait.

> Hikers in 2011 praised pump filters for being dependable and producing taste-free water.

Couples. Pump filters are somewhat convenient for couples as water can be continuously pumped from one water bottle to the next without stopping. It can be a lot of pumping, though.

Organisms removed. Protozoa and bacteria are removed. (A few models treat viruses, but they are either too heavy or incorporate a chemical. See "combining treatments" on page 71.)

Gravity filters

Gravity filters are often dubbed "the lazy person's filter." Stigma aside, though, they take a lot of work out of treating water. Rather than pumping by hand, you scoop water into a bag containing the filter, hang it, and the water drains through a filter into a container below.

Setup and maintenance. Just like the pump filter, the gravity filter and its hose(s) need to be periodically cleaned. Because you need to hang gravity filters, the absence of a suitable tree or rock outcropping may add time to setup. Thus, in some locations, hanging a gravity filter may take creativity.

> Distance hikers are nothing if not creative. I've never encountered a place near water where I couldn't find a place to hang my gravity filter.

Convenience. Its convenience makes the gravity filter attractive for many people. You don't need to babysit it: Just hang the gravity filter and leave it to work on its own while you do other camp chores. This adds to your overall efficiency at camp or simply allows more time to relax and enjoy what's around, rather than fiddling with a pump or mixing chemicals.

In rainstorms, you can leave it hanging while you seek shelter. No more shivering at stream's edge with a pump filter. You do need to check that the container where drinking water flows won't tip over as it fills. It should be easy to stabilize even a collapsible bottle: Wedge it between a few sticks, branches, or rocks. Some models of gravity filters avoid this problem by designing the device so that it can be directly connected to a water bottle. This, however, adds weight to the system. As with the pump filter, you can filter water in whatever quantities you need rather than fixed quantities.

Weight. Carrying weights of gravity filters sold by big box outdoor retailers are comparable to the weights of pump filters. However, owing to their greater simplicity of design, gravity filters are sometimes made and sold by smaller manufacturers who cater more to long-distance or ultralight hikers. Using lightweight materials like silnylon, small manufacturers can cut the weight of a gravity filter to nearly half that of their rivals. There are also a number of do-it-yourself plans online.

Price. Costing between $50 and $110 to treat 500 quarts, gravity filters sold at big box retailers approximate the cost of pump filters. Gravity filters have the same expensive filter replacement issues as pump filters, but are less likely to break when dropped, owing to less plastic housing. Small manufacturers are likely to sell their gravity filters for a few bucks less than big box retailers, and do-it-yourselfers will realize even bigger savings.

Taste. Unaltered.

Time to potability. Water is ready to drink as soon as it passes through the filter.

Couples. Gravity filters carry a distinct advantage over pump filters and UV light because you can make large quantities of water with little effort. This is advantageous for couples as pumping for two or stirring multiple 1-liter quantities of water with a UV pen can be time-consuming and tedious.

Organisms removed. Protozoa and bacteria. Some brands also treat viruses, but they are heavier, flow more slowly, and cost substantially more than filters that do not treat viruses. This is in part due to the extremely small pore size needed for a virus-treating filter. These models are not conducive to long-distance backpacking unless you are traveling where the probability of encountering a virus is high.

Inline filters

Instead of being separate like other technologies, inline filters typically attach directly to a water bottle—you scoop water into the bottle and attach the filter to its top. Because the actual filter outlet resides in the bottle's top, you can drink the water straight from the bottle.

Setup and maintenance. In the filter family, inline filters require the least amount of setup as they are simply attached to the top of a water bottle. No hoses or moving parts to worry about. Some models of filter can be cleaned to prolong filter life.

Convenience. Since inline filters normally attach directly to a drinking device and eliminate the need to separately treat water to be consumed, they have an advantage in convenience over other types of water treatment technologies. However, some types of inlines are only designed to be compatible with small wide-mouth water bottles, which generally hold no more than 1 liter. If you need to carry larger quantities of water, such as in deserts or along dry stretches of trail and you don't want to carry a lot of small bottles, you need to carry your unfiltered water in larger bottles and then squeeze it into the small bottle with the filter to drink. Some may view this as an inconvenience since it requires stopping and transferring water. Other models are compatible with the standard screw types found on many large and small collapsible water bottles and soda bottles. You can potentially fill several large bottles with water, cap them, and then simply switch the location of the filter when you finish one bottle and want to drink out of the other. People who prefer to be able to chug water straight from the bottle without impediment may find inline filters inconvenient, since they do not permit this. The four thru-hikers who used inline filters exclusively had this to say about their choice in the 2011 survey:

- Clogged up by the end of the trail—very slow drip.
- Slow gravity filtration when not sucking it through.
- Slow to gravity-feed for filtering for coffee/flavor drinks.
- The time it takes for large amounts of water.

It wasn't all doom and gloom, however. Some positive comments:

- Easy and versatile.
- Never had to think about it, simple, light.
- Always worked, super ultralight.
- Very easy to use.

Weight. When considering the filter and bottle together, inline filters, on average, are about half the weight of conventional pump or gravity filters. Ultralight gravity filters are comparable in weight to inline filters. Some inline designs can be separated from the bottle and you can attach a hose and drink straight from the water source. Used this way, the water system weighs only a few ounces. However, water cannot be captured and stored in this manner.

Price. In addition to their lower weight, inline filters generally cost less than gravity or pump filters. Today you can buy a new inline filter with a bottle for between $30 and $50. Some models last quite a while before the cartridge needs to be replaced. Other models require frequent cartridge replacement, so always consider the cost and availability of replacement cartridges when choosing a brand.

Taste. Unaltered.

Time to potability. Instant.

Couples. Each member of a couple may want to carry their own inline filter or there will be a lot of sharing or squeezing from one bottle to another. Since inline filters are typically half the price and weight of pump filters, it might not be entirely impractical to carry two inline filters. An ultralight gravity filter may be the better filter choice for couples.

Organisms removed. If you want to spend the money and add virus protection, fancier models treated with iodine resin cost just under $200 to treat 500 quarts of water. The inexpensive models do a good job for protozoa and bacteria.

Chemicals

Chemical additives are another popular choice among long-distance hikers. The major advantages to using a chemical over any other type of water treatment are twofold.

1. *Weight and volume:* Carrying weights of chemical bottles or tabs range from less than an ounce to just over five ounces. They take up very little pack space.
2. *No hassle:* There is nothing to set up or maintain. Simply take out the bottle or tab of chemical, measure the correct amount, drop it into water, and wait.

Long-distance hikers who want to prioritize traveling fast and light above all else may want to consider chemicals. However, there are a few significant downsides to using chemicals.

1. *Time to potability:* Because time is needed for chemicals to act thoroughly, water treated with chemicals cannot be consumed immediately and you may need to wait up to four hours for effective treatment for all potentially harmful waterborne pathogens. The effectiveness of chemicals also depends on the water temperature. That is, they require higher dosages or more time in colder weather.
2. *Health hazards:* Some chemicals carry health risks if used long term.
3. *Taste:* While some chemicals are more noticeable than others, most have a detectable taste.
4. *Rationing:* The amount of water that you can make potable is limited by the amount of chemical you have. This is especially pertinent for chemicals in tablet form, which are expensive. Chemicals in tablet form may need to be carried in larger quantities in locations with hot temperatures and steep terrain, where you need to drink more water. This is less of an issue for cheap chemicals like chlorine bleach that can make a large quantity of water potable with small amounts.

The following is a description of the chemicals most commonly used to treat water in the backcountry. Please note that discussions surrounding the pros and cons of various chemicals for water treatment can be highly technical and complex. It is not the aim of this book to delve extensively into the chemistry of each type of treatment. For practical long-distance hiking, the information in the following pages will allow you to make a sound choice.

Chlorine bleach

Chlorine bleach is possibly the simplest and least expensive water purification method available. Basic bleach is essentially a solution of sodium hypochlorite and water, which react to form sodium hydroxide and an electrically neutral chlorine compound called hypochlorous acid, which either destroys waterborne pathogens or makes them incapable of reproduction.

Setup and maintenance. Chemicals don't rely on a device or anything with moving parts for delivery, so there's no maintenance. Setup simply means measuring out the proper amount of bleach based on the amount of water to be treated and the air temperature.

Convenience. While it certainly seems convenient to put a few drops of bleach in water, the process of

Fluke or trend? Of the 85 thru-hikers who finished and took the 2011 survey, 25 (29 percent) reported using bleach. This made bleach the most popular choice for treating water.

using bleach isn't so straightforward. Since commercially prepared chlorine bleach does not contain a uniform amount of chlorine, dosage depends on the type of bleach you use. Additionally, some brands of bleach do not specify the exact amount of chlorine contained in the solution. There are also several other factors, such as temperature and pH, that alter the efficacy of bleach. To be more precise in dosing bleach, it may be useful to purchase or mix a bleach product with an exact known concentration of chlorine.

> The materials safety data sheet (MSDS) for Clorox bleach notes that concentrations of sodium hypochlorite range from 5 to 10 percent.

Weight. A bottle containing 50mL of 5 percent chlorine bleach (enough for 500 quarts) weighs approximately 3 ounces, depending on the size and composition of the bottle. This is extraordinarily lightweight.

Price. A large bottle of bleach costs $2, making it the least expensive water treatment method available.

Taste. Assuredly noticeable.

Time to potability. Depends on water temperature.

Couples. Chlorine bleach is economical and practical for couples.

Health hazards. There are no known health hazards to using bleach to disinfect water at appropriate concentrations.

Organisms removed. Protozoa (except *Cryptosporidium*), bacteria, and viruses. Technically, with long enough contact (days), chlorine can kill *Cryptosporidium*, but this is impractical for long-distance hiking.

Time to Treat Water at pH 5.5–7.5 with Chlorine Bleach

Water temperature (°F)	Time to wait after treatment (minutes)
>64	30
50	60
At or just above 32	120

Dosage of Chlorine Bleach Needed to Treat 1L of Water

Percent sodium hypochlorite in bleach	Drops per liter of water
2	5
5	2
10	1

Calculations are based on an effective dosage of 5.0mg chlorine per liter of water and a standard drop size of 0.05mL.

Chlorine dioxide

Chlorine dioxide is widely considered to be more potent than chlorine bleach for inactivating waterborne pathogens. It has also been reported to be better at penetrating biofilms, which are living structures in the water where most bacteria are thought to reside. It's also considered to be better tasting. Chlorine dioxide is sold in tablet or liquid form by most major retailers under several different brand names.

Setup and maintenance. Chlorine dioxide in tablet form does not require setup. In liquid form you need to mix two separate solutions before you add them to water.

Convenience. Like most chemical compounds, chlorine dioxide in tab or liquid form can be dropped into water without much hassle. An inconvenience, shared by all chemicals, is that chlorine dioxide requires a waiting period before water is safe to drink. Waiting periods for commercially made chlorine dioxide tabs are based on the type of waterborne pathogen for which coverage is desired.

If you need to cover *Cryptosporidium*, treatment time can take an inconvenient four hours. Treatment time is also longer for very cold water since the efficiency of chlorine dioxide decreases with temperature.

Weight. A package of chloride dioxide tabs weighs less than an ounce. In liquid form, chlorine dioxide drops weigh between 2 and 4 ounces. Both are extremely light, and users of chlorine dioxide in 2011 frequently cited the light weight along with taste as being what they liked best about chlorine dioxide.

Price. Cost depends on whether chlorine dioxide is tablet or liquid form. In liquid form, chlorine dioxide costs between $30 and $60 per 500 quarts of water, depending on what size you carry. Chlorine dioxide tabs are far more expensive. Treating 500 quarts costs over $200 and, for some sizes and brands, over $300. This might be because tabs are rated to cover a wider range of waterborne pathogens than liquid.

Wait Times for Chlorine Dioxide Tabs and Mixed Oxidants	
Organism	**Wait times**
Viruses and bacteria	15 minutes
Giardia (protozoa)	30 minutes
Cryptosporidium (protozoa)	4 hours

Treating for *Cryptosporidium* is a personal decision. If you plan on traveling through areas where water sources are likely to be contaminated by people or animals (e.g., high-use areas, pastures), then the risk of acquiring *Cryptosporidium* is higher than if you travel through more sparse or protected areas. If you don't feel as though you can accept any risk or don't want to wait four hours for effective treatment, then choosing another water treatment technology is advised, since most chemicals do not cover *Cryptosporidium*.

Taste. Chlorine dioxide is much less noticeable than chlorine bleach or liquid iodine. In fact, chlorine dioxide is sometimes used to improve the taste of stale water. Nonetheless, chloride dioxide is still a chemical additive and will alter the taste, for better or for worse.

Time to potability. Depends on the temperature of the water and the pathogen coverage you want.

Couples. Using chlorine dioxide tabs can get expensive for couples. Couples also have to be sure to carry at least two packs of tabs to have enough water to drink on an average stretch of trail during a long-distance hike. Chlorine dioxide in liquid form is more cost feasible, and a single bottle of solution will last a couple through multiple resupply points. Since tabs weigh about a third as much as liquid, there isn't much weight difference between carrying lots of tabs and a single bottle of liquid.

Health hazards. There are no known health hazards to using chlorine dioxide to disinfect water at appropriate concentrations.

Organisms removed. Chlorine dioxide tabs can destroy protozoa, bacteria, and viruses. Chlorine dioxide in liquid form has been rated only for bacteria because it is a weaker solution than tabs. Tripling or quadrupling the amount of liquid chlorine dioxide used per liter could theoretically match the coverage level of tabs, but this would have a negative impact on cost and convenience.

Iodine

In the backpacking community over recent years, iodine has taken a bit of a backseat to chlorine dioxide, possibly because iodine does not destroy *Cryptosporidium*. It may also be due to iodine's noticeable taste and its tendency to tint clear water bottles. Nonetheless, considering that chlorine dioxide tabs take a tedious four hours to destroy *Cryptosporidium*, practically speaking, iodine may be just as useful as chlorine dioxide tabs for long-distance hiking. Iodine is most commonly sold in tablet or aqueous crystal form under several brand names.

Setup and maintenance. Tablets don't require any setup or maintenance. Aqueous crystals need a small amount of water for preparing a solution. The solution takes one hour to be ready. Usually you can prepare the solution well in advance of when you need the water.

Convenience. Aqueous crystal dosage must be adjusted based on the temperature of the water. Colder temperatures require a higher dosage of solution. This can easily become an inconvenience in cold-weather travel.

Weight. Carrying weight for tabs or crystals is approximately 3 ounces.

Price. Iodine in aqueous crystal form is cheaper than most other technologies. Iodine tabs are also price-competitive with 500 quarts of water treated for between $120 and $140. This, however, doesn't come close to spending less than $20 for aqueous crystals.

Taste. A drawback of iodine for many people. One version of iodine tabs comes with a second group of tabs to control taste.

Time to potability. Twenty minutes for aqueous crystals once added to water. (This does not include the 1-hour mixture preparation time.) For tabs, you need to wait 30 minutes.

> One 2011 hiker writes, "[Iodine was] cheap and effective. We used Polar Pure and it lasted the whole trail."

Couples. Unless you are traveling in consistently warm weather where water is plentiful, each member of a couple should carry his or her own iodine. In cold weather, you need to mix additional solution for the aqueous crystal form. The amount of premixed solution from one bottle is not likely to be enough for two people to use at once. Also, along trails where water is scarce and you need to carry multiple liters, you may need to treat more water at once than you can mix the amount of solution for. There are ways of getting around this, but it adds inconvenience. For tabs, a single bottle is able to treat 25 quarts, which is barely enough for two people on a four- to six-day outing.

Health hazards. Iodine is an essential component in regulation of the human thyroid gland. Excessive ingestion of iodine may be related to decreased thyroid function, although this has not been definitively proven in research. Nonetheless, sound science recommends that iodine not be used for periods longer than three months or by people with a history of thyroid disease, a strong family history of thyroid disease, or a hypersensitivity to iodine.

Organisms removed. Bacteria, viruses, and protozoa (except *Cryptosporidia*).

Mixed oxidants

Mixed oxidants can be used for disinfecting water. Mixed oxidants are produced after sending an electrical current through salt water. A commercially available pen-shaped device called the MIOX does just this. Unfortunately, Cascade Designs, the manufacturer of the MIOX, has discontinued production as of this publication. However, the MIOX can still be purchased on the secondary market. This nifty handheld device is lightweight and portable, adding a clever twist to the market for chemical water treatment.

Setup and maintenance. Setup is fairly minimal. Salt and water need to first be added to the device to make a solution. The solution is then treated with an electrical current to make a treatment solution for a fixed amount of water. Field maintenance of the device includes changing the batteries and restocking the safety indicator strips.

Convenience. Like all other forms of chemical treatment, mixed oxidants require time to treat. Times for mixed oxidants are the same as chlorine dioxide tabs (see page 72). Mixed oxidants require an additional series of steps where pH indicator strips are applied to ensure proper water pH. If you don't get the proper pH, you need to make more solution. And because the MIOX is battery operated, you will need to preheat it for it to perform well in near-freezing or subfreezing air temperatures. On the plus side, you don't have to pump it or fiddle with hoses. Once the solution is made it can be set aside to rest while the wait time expires.

Weight. The weight of the device, batteries, salt, and test strips approximates 8 ounces, clearly the heaviest of all chemical treatments, but comparable to ultralight gravity filters.

Price. Costing between $160 and $180 to treat 500 quarts, the device isn't cheap, but it's far less than chlorine dioxide tabs and on par with some filters and the solar version of the UV pen.

Taste. Definitely noticeable salty taste.

Time to potability. Similar to chlorine dioxide. Add a bit more time if you need to make multiple solutions.

Couples. The MIOX purports to make up to 4 liters at once with the capability of making another 4 liters without needing to wait for another solution to be ready. It can make as much water as the battery life and available salt allow, so you do not need to ration tabs. Mixed oxidants are thus more practical for couples than aqueous iodine crystals or chlorine dioxide tabs, but not chlorine bleach or filters.

Health hazards. There are no known health hazards to using mixed oxidants.

Organisms removed. Bacteria, protozoa, viruses.

Ultraviolet light

Ultraviolet (UV) light is in a league of its own when it comes to treating wilderness water for safe consumption. This is because it can effectively treat bacteria, protozoa, and viruses without long wait times or lots of setup and maintenance. The device is typically pen shaped and delivers pulses of UV light that distort the DNA and RNA of living organisms in the water being treated, rendering them incapable of reproduction and therefore harmless.

UV light was used by 12 percent of thru-hikers completing the survey in 2011. The most popular water treatment method was bleach, used by 29 percent.

Over the past ten years, UV light has become an increasingly popular form of water treatment among long-distance hikers, perhaps because unlike the market for filters and chemicals, the UV market is not yet saturated with competing technologies and brands. Also, UV has the capacity to treat all classes of waterborne pathogens: protozoa, bacteria, and viruses. It does so with comparatively less hassle than filters and chemicals.

This doesn't mean that UV light is necessarily a slam dunk when it comes to treating backcountry water. Just like any technology, UV light has inconveniences, and hikers who wish to use UV have to consider these in accordance with their own preferences and style. While not quite as popular as filters and chemicals, UV now has a strong following among long-distance hikers and will likely remain a strong alternative for years to come.

The UV pen is currently the only form of UV light suitable for long-distance hiking. UV pens are sold as is or built to link with a specially designed bottle. There are other methods of delivering UV light, such as hand crank models and bottle-top devices, but these are bulkier and/or heavier than the battery-powered pens.

Setup and maintenance. The UV pen simply needs to be removed from its case. Like chemicals, UV pens are virtually maintenance free. The lamp of the pen will eventually need replacing, but this is not typically a trail-maintenance issue. Lamps typically last 8,000 to 10,000 treatments.

Convenience. Convenience is a strong selling feature of UV pens. There is definite appeal to pulling out the pen, pressing a button, stirring or shaking, and having totally purified, taste-free water in less than two minutes. The modern UV pen eliminates a lot of the hassle associated with setting up hoses, scrubbing filters, waiting for chemicals to be ready, and so on. However, there are some notable inconveniences associated with the UV pen:

- *Batteries:* Dying or dead batteries in the midst of treating water is a hassle and it's difficult to predict when this may happen, so always bring a spare set. Dead batteries are even more of a hassle when using the solar-rechargeable models, whose batteries don't last as long. Also, hikers who travel in dense forest or are under cloud cover for long periods of time will have more frequent solar-rechargeable battery issues.
- *Small quantities:* Modern models of the UV pen are only capable of treating up to one liter at a time. On trails like the southern California section of the PCT, where there are such long distances between reliable water sources that you sometimes need to treat many liters of water in one place, the UV pen user will need to sit and stir each liter. This is especially inconvenient for couples.
- *Cold weather:* Because the UV pen is battery powered, it is likely to experience performance problems in colder weather.
- *No narrow-mouth bottles:* The pen-shaped device does not fit in narrow-mouthed water bottle openings. Many collapsible water bottles, popular with distance hikers due to their low weight and pack volume, feature this type of design. UV pen users will either need to carry wide-mouth bottles or first treat water in cook pots before transferring to narrow-mouthed bottles.
- *Prefiltering:* You need to prefilter water treated by UV pens if the water is murky, significantly turbid, or has floating organic matter. You can use a bandana or buy a prefilter. It's important to note that consistently treating water that is murky or contains suspended particles will add inconvenience to any type of water treatment technology.

Convenience and taste were the things the ten thru-hikers who used UV and completed the 2011 survey liked the most about the technology. Comments about UV light are as follows:

- Fast and easy.
- Quick, easy to use.
- Ease of use.
- Very easy and reliable.
- Small, lightweight. Very convenient since there was no waiting time. Could fill a bottle at a stream, drink it, then fill again and leave. Can't do the same with chemical treatments.
- Fast, easy, fun in the dark.
- Instant and did not change the taste of the water.

- Quick and no chemicals.
- Easy, tasteless, instant.
- Fast and tasteless.

Then again, the inconvenience of batteries was what the ten hikers listed as the most common dislike:

- Nothing.
- Batteries didn't last long.
- Hard to see when the treatment is finished.
- Nothing.
- Had to always carry extra batteries.
- Batteries.
- Batteries. I did start using 0.5L battery power to treat 1L to conserve batteries and neither one of us got sick.
- Batteries.
- Running out of battery.
- Weight.

Weight. Models that use disposable batteries are as light as 3.6 ounces with batteries. Add an ounce for spare batteries to round the total package to nearly 5 ounces. This is lighter than virtually all filters and a few ounces heavier than chemicals. The solar rechargeable and pen-bottle models come in a good bit heavier, owing to the weight of the charging device or bottle. Weights can be as high as 12 ounces.

Price. The cost to treat 500 quarts of water while operating a disposable or USB rechargeable battery model comes in just under $120, which includes the device's purchase price. The solar-rechargeable model has a mostly flat cost, which is its initial purchase cost of $149.99. The only foreseeable future costs with both models are replacement lamps ($20) and replacing batteries. Lamps are capable of 8,000 to 10,000 treatments. Solar rechargeable batteries are capable of taking 300 charges until you need to replace the batteries, which makes quite a bit of water. The rechargeable model is financially advantageous for extended use on multiple trails. Of course, because it's a device powered by electricity with a glass bulb at one end, there is inherent risk of being dropped on a rock and broken. This might increase the cost for some people. UV pens typically come with protective cases.

Time to potability. One liter of water takes about 1½ minutes to treat, after which it is immediately ready to drink.

Couples. Because current models of UV pens can only treat up to one liter at a time, they are not ideally suited for couples.

Health hazards. Modern UV pens are safe to use and will automatically shut off if taken out of the water.

Organisms treated. Viruses, bacteria, and protozoa.

Combining treatments

The technologies for treating water in the backcountry are varied and often complex. Whether it's the number of organisms treated, cost, weight, taste, or any other consideration, filters, chemicals, and UV light each have their own strengths and drawbacks. For this reason, some hikers combine technologies to get the best of both worlds. When done right, combining technologies can be a way to treat backcountry water worry and hassle free without putting too big a dent in the bank account.

It makes the most sense to combine technologies when you want to cover bacteria, protozoa, and viruses. You can do this by combining a filter with a chemical. (UV light already covers all three classes of waterborne pathogen, so combining it with another technology just adds hassle.) There are two ways of combining technology: ready-made and do-it-yourself.

Ready-made. Some manufacturers have engineered filters that interface with a chemical. The most common is a pump filter coated with an iodine resin. The filter effectively removes larger protozoa and bacteria from the drinking water and the iodine resin treats the virus. The advantage of iodine resin is that it doesn't typically leave an iodine taste in the water and doesn't carry the health risks that iodine in tablet or drop form does when used over the long term. This is because resin is a much more stable form of iodine and doesn't dissolve easily in water.

Do-it-yourself. A more economical way of achieving a filter-chemical hybrid is to use a filter with drops of chlorine bleach (see previous section for dosage). This method covers all waterborne pathogens since the filter blocks protozoa and bacteria while the bleach kills the viruses. Many longtime backpackers have adopted this strategy, although the technique does not yet seem to be widely

> Only 2 of 85 finishing thru-hikers in the 2011 survey reported mixing a filter and a chemical to treat water.

spread through the long-distance hiking community. It's certainly an ultralight approach, as a 2-ounce inline filter can be combined with a 3-ounce bottle of bleach to make a highly effective water treatment system weighing less than half a pound. This system is less advantageous in near-freezing temperatures, where the wait time for bleach approaches two hours.

Water Treatment Cross Technology Comparison
(devices weighing >16 oz. excluded)

Technology	Weight (oz.)	Cost to Treat 500 Qt. (USD)	Virus	Bacteria	Protozoa	Wait Time after Treatment (min.)	Comments
Chlorine Bleach	3.00	$2.00	☒	☒	☒ (except *Cryptosporidium*)	30–120	Wait time depends on water temperature and pH 5.5–7.5.
Chlorine Dioxide Tabs	0.4–0.9	$220–$330	☒	☒	☒	Up to 240 for Crypto coverage	Longer wait for cold water and Crypto
Chlorine Dioxide Drops	2.00–4.00	$30–$60	☐	☒	☐	15–20	
Iodine Tabs	3.00	$120–$140	☒	☒	☒ (except *Cryptosporidium*)	30	Health risks for long-term use
Iodine Crystals	3.00	$15–$20	☒	☒	☒ (except *Cryptosporidium*)	20	1 hour mix time before treatment; health risks for long-term use
Mixed Oxidants	4.9 (includes spare batteries)	$160–$180	☒	☒	☒	Up to 240 for Crypto coverage	Longer wait for cold water and Crypto
Pump Filters	7.40–16.00	$70–$370	☐*	☒	☒	none	* Select models treat viruses
Gravity Filters	7.75–12.00	$50.00–$110	☐	☒	☒	none	
Inline Filters	2.00–9.70	$50–$190	☐*	☒	☒	none	* Select models treat viruses
UV Devices	5.20–12.00 (weight with batteries)	$115.00–$150	☒	☒	☒	none	

Cost figures are based on prices at time of publication and include replacement batteries and filters where appropriate.

Shelter

As a beginner preparing for the Appalachian Trail in 2002, I thought choosing a shelter was exclusively about which kind of tent to buy. The big local outfitter near our house didn't offer any alternatives to a tent, and I wasn't experienced enough to know any better. So trying my best to be conscious of weight and volume, I picked out a single-wall, one-person structure. The tent held up nicely, but I mailed it home when I got to Virginia. I recall the recipient of that particular package having a bit of a worry upon opening the box and seeing my tent enclosed with some dirty socks. A quick phone call was enough to reassure that yes, I was still alive, had clean socks, and no, was not digging a hole in the ground to sleep in. I had simply decided to get rid of the tent and hop along from shelter to shelter.

Tents are still widely considered by the mainstream to be the go-to shelter structure for backpacking, but there have always been acceptable alternatives. The difference between today and ten years ago is that alternatives to tents now occupy a noticeable commercial niche, although tents

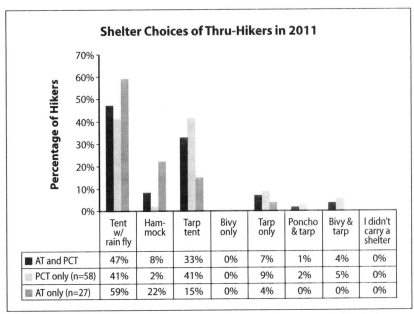

	Tent w/ rain fly	Ham-mock	Tarp tent	Bivy only	Tarp only	Poncho & tarp	Bivy & tarp	I didn't carry a shelter
■ AT and PCT	47%	8%	33%	0%	7%	1%	4%	0%
PCT only (n=58)	41%	2%	41%	0%	9%	2%	5%	0%
■ AT only (n=27)	59%	22%	15%	0%	4%	0%	0%	0%

The 85 hikers who finished the AT or PCT in 2011 reported which kind of shelter they carried for more than 75 percent of the trail. Surprisingly, none of the AT hikers went without a shelter, but this may just be because of the low sample size.

still make up the bulk of floor space at large outdoor retailers (shreds of Tyvek just don't carry the profit margins). However, if you happen to attend a long-distance hiker's conference like an ALDHA gathering or Trail Days, which are far less hindered by sales pressures, you'll see all sorts of non-tent shelters. I'm not trying to dissuade anyone from purchasing a tent. However, having an open mind and being aware of alternatives to tents is definitely well worth the time and money. The diversity of shelters used by thru-hikers on the AT and PCT is now quite evident.

Before deciding which kind of shelter suits you best, you might first want to decide if carrying a shelter is even necessary for the trip you're planning. One trail that can be hiked without a shelter in tow is the AT. The AT features a network of fixed structures, most of which have three walls, a roof, and fit six to eight hikers comfortably. With a few exceptions, this shelter system is available free of charge for the entire length of the AT. Spacing of the shelters is variable, but the average thru-hiker will likely encounter around two each day. The downsides to using the shelter system in lieu of a portable shelter are lack of privacy, rodent infestation of some shelters, inflexibility of itinerary, and overcrowding during peak season. Overcrowding can be a source of real consternation between backpackers, especially among the masses that set forth from Georgia's Springer Mountain each spring. Although good AT shelter etiquette dictates that room is made for all comers and large groups camp away from shelters, not everyone is so accommodating, especially in bad weather.

Essential considerations

If you've decided to go on a long-distance hiking trip carrying a portable shelter, there are plenty of options that will fit your style and preferences. There are five main categories of portable shelter: tent, tarp tent, bivy, tarp, and hammock. Each category of shelter is capable of keeping the rain and the bugs out. However, they each do so to varying degrees and some perform better than others in certain environments. In choosing what type of shelter might suit you best, there are a number of key factors to consider:

Environment. Both a tent and a bivy will provide shelter in virtually any environment without much thought as to how they are pitched. This is the great advantage of these designs. Many tent and bivy users can plop down on a rocky, treeless summit without needing to worry about much more than strong winds. A tarp user, on the other hand, not only has to locate suitable structures from which to string the tarp, but also has to put a little more thought into the direction of the wind and the geographic makeup of the camp location. Tarp users who don't carry some sort of bug netting have to avoid calm, wet areas on warm nights if they don't want to be constantly harassed by mosquitoes. The same awareness should be paid to loose, sandy soil where ants like to live. Ants in the sleeping bag equals no sleep whatsoever. Hammock users have similar environmental considerations as tarp users, without the hassles of insects.

Couples. Tents can provide a significant source of warmth for couples. Because they are fully enclosed, tents do a good job at trapping radiant heat, so two people sharing a tent might be able to get away with carrying sleeping bags rated at warmer temperatures.

> What's a tarp tent? Among shelter manufacturers, definitions and styles vary from semi-structured tarps to fully enclosed shelters. For the purposes of this book, a tarp tent is any structured shelter designed to be used without a rain fly. A tent is a structured, fully enclosed shelter designed to be used with a rain fly.

Weight, cost, and pack volume. While there are certainly exceptions, tents, as a category, tend to be heavier, more expensive, and take up more pack space than other shelter types. However, when a tent is shared by a couple, weight and cost considerations become competitive with other shelter types.

Comfort. Hammock aficionados will tell you that sleeping in a hammock is more comfortable than sleeping on the ground. This is debatable. Try a hammock before you commit. Tents, tarp tents, and tarps top the legroom category.

Impact. Hammock users also claim that because they are suspended above the ground, hammocks are more in keeping with leave-no-trace wilderness ethics. The truth is that while hammocks certainly don't leave a ground print behind, careful tenters, tarpers, and biviers alike can do a good job minimizing impact by choosing durable surfaces to sleep on.

Aesthetics. How much do you value simplicity versus complexity? Old school versus high tech? Having walls and a ceiling versus being "closer to nature"? The shelter type that tends to be more high tech and laden with features is the tent. (There aren't a lot of ads for simple tarps in backpacking magazines.) If you are a technophobe, ardent minimalist, don't need much privacy, and don't mind the stomping, scurrying, scratching, and squeaking that might happen inches from or right on your head at night, then you may want to lean toward a bivy or a tarp. If you love the wilderness during the day, but prefer the security of an enclosure at night, then you might want to lean toward a tent, tarp tent, or a hammock.

The rest of this section is dedicated to guiding the decision-making process for choosing a shelter in each of the five major design categories. The market for shelters is huge and can be thoroughly confusing, so read on!

Tent

If you've decided on a tent, you've still got a bit of work to do. The amount that could be written on the different styles and features of modern tents could fill the cinder cone of Mt. St. Helens. The good news is that the basic structural and material elements that determine what constitutes an effective tent have been figured out. Look through gear catalogs and magazines and you'll see a lot of variation on what is essentially the same tried and true tent design. Modern backpacking tents are oval, rectangular, or trapezoidal in shape, maintain a low profile to the ground, and have a system of quick-to-set-up ultralight poles and guy lines. Rain flys are made of lightweight, waterproof material. No modern, two-person tent should take more than five minutes to set up or weigh more than 6 pounds. Any major deviation from these features usually results in a tent that looks interesting but fails the user in any number of categories ranging from weatherproofing to weight to quality and durability. The tents that consistently get the best ratings from users are the ones that don't stray too far from the basics.

The bad news is that in order to distinguish themselves from their competitors but still make good tents, manufacturers need to emphasize the minute details. This means that you, the interested tent shopper, will be confronted with dozens of oddly spelled proprietary fabrics, mountains of industry jargon, and the assumption that you have a basic working knowledge of thermodynamics. It's easy to get caught up in discussions about things like membrane permeability and clip design and forget the basics when it comes to tent shopping. It's not that the minute things are unimportant, it's just that they are some of the last things to look at after you make other, more important decisions and narrow the choices to just a handful of models. So, then, a framework for deciding on a tent:

Price. Starting here will either narrow down the field considerably or do absolutely nothing. In today's dollars, a new, high-quality, lightweight, three-season backpacking tent costs between $200 and $400. While expensive, tents in this price range will last quite a long time if properly taken care of. High-end, bombproof, and ultra-lightweight tents cost upward of $500. Tents in this price range are definitely top quality, but they are not essential for three-season backpacking. Be cautious of new tents retailing for $150 or less. Chances are that tents this cheap are made from inferior materials and methods and will fail under harsh weather conditions. If your budget is this low, you may want to look into another shelter design. You'll get a low-quality tent for $150, but you'll get a high-quality tarp or bivy with some cash to spare.

Size and shape. If you're tall or if you're going to be sharing a tent with a partner, take that into consideration. Most tents list the length and width of the sleeping space. I have found 57 inches (145 cm) of width to be a pretty snug fit for two average-sized people. You might also want to consider whether you want your door or doors oriented in the front and back or along the sides. If you aren't quite so limber, you may want to seek out a tent that permits entry from the side(s).

Freestanding or staked. You can set up freestanding tents without pounding stakes into the ground. The advantage of the freestanding design is that it is fast to set up, can be moved without disassembly, and can be pitched anywhere. Having owned both freestanding and staked tents, I have found that the ability to pick up and move a tent without disassembling it is a fantastic feature. I also enjoy the versatility of being able to plop a tent down on rocks, loose sand, or other terrain where stakes would be impossible. This kind of versatility is, after all, one of the big reasons for choosing a tent in the first place. Staked tents have the advantage of being a bit lighter because they have fewer poles. You can judge the weight versus convenience for yourself. Most freestanding tents still need a few stakes if the rain fly is in use.

Reviews and features. Hopefully you've been able to narrow the choices down to five models or fewer. Now is the time to ponder clip types, stash pockets, and different space-age fabrics. To get a real sense for how everything performs, go online and see what people have to say. Read a few user reviews on your choices. When reading reviews, try to first read from websites or publications that aren't in the business of selling tents or selling advertising to the manufacturers of the tents under re-

> You can read user reviews on backpack geartest.org and backpackinglight.com. Both have extensive reader content on different types of backpacking equipment.

view. A good reviewer will comment on the water resistance of the tent and will hopefully have tested the tent in stormy weather. Such a reviewer will also discuss durability, insect proofing, condensation, secondary features, and ease of setup.

Warranty. Make sure the manufacturer or outfitter offers a good warranty. This is specifically important for tents, since they are expensive and some critical, breakable parts like poles cannot be easily replaced. I have, in the course of covering many miles of trail, broken more than a few tent poles. I have been thankful that in each case, I could get on the phone, call the manufacturer, and have new poles shipped to my next mail drop free of charge.

Tarp tent

The tarp tent fills the gap between traditional tents and simple tarps. Tarp tents come in many designs. Some more closely resemble tents in form and function, featuring poles and stakes. Some have full separation between the floor and the walls while others are fully enclosed. Other tarp tents are more closely related to tarps, featuring a single piece of waterproof fabric and perhaps offering space for a trekking pole support to add more structure.

Tarp tents have become increasingly popular on the long-distance trails of the United States, maybe because the tarp tent combines the desirable features of a tent (bug-proofing, weatherproofing on all sides) with the desirable features of a tarp (lightweight, airy, less expensive) to make a shelter that seems to truly be the best of both worlds. Naturally, there are a few drawbacks.

First, because many tarp tents are essentially tents with fewer structural components, they can be more vulnerable in high winds, so tarp tent users need to be a bit more cautious about campsite location.

According to 2011 survey results, tarp tents were popular along the PCT, where they were equal in numbers compared to traditional tents. They don't seem to have caught on as much along the rainier AT, where tents significantly outnumbered tarp tents.

Second, the style of tarp tent that is fully enclosed, similar to a traditional tent, has a single-wall design. This design foregoes a separate rain fly and instead relies on highly water-resistant, breathable material to double as the main shelter structure and the weatherproofing. The primary advantages of the single-wall design over the tent-and-separate-rainfly design are that it is usually much lighter and takes up less pack space. A word of caution here: Virtually no fabric is 100 percent waterproof and breathable in all conditions. With single-wall designs, it's important to read the fine print and ignore the hype. Few fabrics used in single-wall designs even claim to be waterproof. Most are water resistant, meaning that the fabric will repel water most of the time but might leak in a deluge. Users of single-wall tarp tents may therefore want to take care that they camp near terrain features such as thick stands of trees, which take the brunt of storms and will ensure that the tent wall doesn't get pounded by rain.

There's nothing worse than sitting up on a cold morning, bumping your head on the tent wall, and getting showered with freezing cold water. The other knock against single-wall tarp tents is that they are prone to condensation. Manufacturers of tarp tents know this and take measures to carefully engineer around the problem. To reduce condensation, traditional tents are made with copious amounts of mesh to provide ventilation and reduce moisture buildup. A separate external rain fly that does not contact the tent provides the weatherproofing. Because they don't have rain flys, single-wall tarp tents must incorporate strategically placed small vents and flaps embedded in the wall material to achieve adequate ventilation, but also adequate weatherproofing. It's never a perfect solution, and condensation tends to bother tarp tent users more so than traditional tent-with-rain-fly users.

The graph below provides a comparison between tarp tent and tarp users who answered the question, "What did you like the least about your

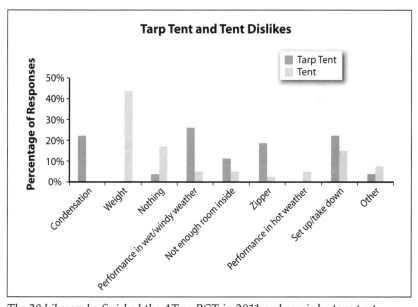

The 28 hikers who finished the AT or PCT in 2011 and carried a tarp tent provided a total of 29 responses. The 40 hikers who carried a tent provided a total of 41 responses.

shelter?" Tarp tent users were most dissatisfied with wet or windy weather performance by a few percentage points, but there was a fairly wide distribution of problems. Tent users were overwhelmingly disappointed with weight and had far fewer other problems. More tent users seemed happy with their choice, judging by the fact that 17 percent of their responses were "nothing" or "n/a" compared to 4 percent of tarp tent users.

The decision to go with either of these two popular shelter models, tent and tarp tent, boils down to a basic set of pros and cons:

	Tent	Tarp tent
Pros	weatherproof and bug proof	lightweight
Cons	heavy	condensation, not weatherproof in hard rain, zippers

Don't expect to find tarp tents at any major land-based retailers. Tarp tents still occupy the realm of the small, semiobscure boutique manufacturer, although there are now a few household names. Tracking down tarp tent manufacturers isn't difficult, and a quick internet search provides plenty of good hits. If the opportunity comes up, try out a tarp tent at a long-distance hiker's conference like an ALDHA gathering, the Pacific Crest Trail Annual Day Zero Kick Off (PCTADZKO), or Trail Days in Damascus, Virginia. Otherwise, go online and read what independent reviewers have to say.

Tarp

Three species of hikers habitually sleep under tarps. One is the creaky Old Crock whose 7- by 11-foot war-surplus life-raft sail is enshrined in memory with his Model A and who always has felt tents are for (1) winter, (2) nights in the summit crater of Mt. Rainier, and (3) girls. The second is neither cranky nor old but has been on the trails long enough to comprehend that tent-campers are retreaters-to-the-womb, that tarp-campers, livers-with-nature, intimately know not only the wind and bugs but also sights of moonlit clouds and shooting stars and dawn, scents of pine needles and flowers and grasses and prowling skunks, sounds of little feet scurrying in the darkness over sleeping bags and faces. They experience more of everything except claustrophobia, and in retrospect their wilderness nights are as memorable as their days. The third tarper is the beginning backpacker who compares weights and prices and decides (shrewd chap) that tents are for rich donkeys.

–Harvey Manning, *Backpacking: One Step at a Time*

My first experience with a tarp was on the Pacific Crest Trail. The single-wall bivy I was using failed miserably one night in a hailstorm, and with the bulk of the Cascades still to come, I was determined to find a more waterproof solution. As a weight-and-space-conscious solo hiker with limited funds, I didn't want to invest in a tent. So I purchased a single silnylon tarp and some rope, which created a fairly cozy and lightweight shelter that I could sleep and cook under. Still wanting to keep out bugs and for a bit of additional weatherproofing, I also bought a bivy. The combination worked out well, and I made it through the Cascades without much trouble from the weather.

A tarp is just a single sheet of fabric tied up with a rope or a few ropes in a way that keeps its user dry. They've been around for ages. Growing up in Maine, we used them to cover farm equipment, wood, and to insulate the ground if we expected a frost. I'm thinking, of course, of the crinkly blue polyethylene tarps that are so prevalent around farms and ranches. These tarps keep out all

> Silnylon is silicone-impregnated nylon. It is both highly waterproof and lightweight.

types of weather and could probably stop a bullet, although they aren't very lightweight and don't stuff well, and thus are poorly suited for backpacking. Backpacking tarps also do a fine job keeping weather out, but they are usually made of lightweight, packable material, a more common material being silnylon.

Committing to a tarp requires some practice before setting off on the trail because pitching a tarp effectively involves a certain degree of skill. Unlike a tent, which is an unchanging structure, a tarp needs to be set up differently based on terrain and weather conditions. In addition to understanding multiple pitching methods, tarp users should be comfortable getting creative with different-sized trees, branches, rocks, and logs. The payoff for learning to set up a tarp is a considerable reduction in pack weight and volume when compared to carrying any other type of shelter. Since tarps need to be tied up to something, they're not the best choice for a lot of travel over treeless terrain.

There aren't a lot of choices when it comes to tarps, so picking a model is pretty straightforward.

Material. Silnylon is popular. Tyvek, a lightweight form of polyethylene that is waterproof and allows vapor to pass out, is also a good choice.

Size. At the comfortable minimum, a tarp should be a few feet longer than the sleeping bag: 8 x 10 feet is a comfortable size for one person.

Accessories. There aren't many for tarps. Commercially made tarps might come with grommets and bug netting, which are nice. If you're liberating some Tyvek from a nearby construction project, don't expect frills.

Bivy

For certain styles of backpacking, a bivy is an excellent choice. Traditional versions of bivies are structureless enclosures made of weather-resistant, breathable fabric. They usually offer just enough room to accommodate a single person inside a sleeping bag. The bivy is often zipped up over the head and equipped with some type of mesh to allow comfortable breathing at night (this is debatable) and keep the insects out. Some bivy designs feature a single hoop over the head to allow a little more airspace between one's face and the mesh. Other bivies have hoops at the head and foot. The more rugged and weather-resistant bivies minimize mesh over the face and allow breathing at night by way of well-placed vents.

The bivy, perhaps more than any other shelter type, accommodates a highly specific style of travel, one where minimal weight, volume, and rapid speed of shelter deployment take top priority. The bivy is extremely lightweight and can be stuffed down to a tiny ball in the pack. The hoopless designs can be pitched almost instantaneously. There are a few significant caveats to relying on a bivy for a long-distance hike.

Claustrophobia. Bivies are not for those who feel uncomfortable in tight spaces. There is no moving around in a bivy like there is under a tarp or in a tent. Hooped bivies might allow you to prop up on your elbows, but that's about it. Think of zipping yourself up in a body bag every night. That's a bivy. If you require a little more roof or even a wall in your shelter, the bivy might not be the right choice.

Single-wall design. Bivies incorporate the same single-wall tent design as some tarp tents (see tarp tent section). Therefore, in wet environments, users of bivies need to take care that they camp near terrain features such as thick stands of trees, which take the brunt of storms and will ensure that the bivy doesn't get pounded by rain. Most bivies are not weatherproof and will not keep you dry if you are out all night in the pouring rain.

> Only 3 of 85 thru-hikers in the 2011 survey reported using a bivy. All combined the bivy with a tarp.

Although a bivy can technically be pitched anywhere there's a flat surface, it's ill-advised to use a bivy in an exposed area if heavy rains are expected. Also worth noting is that bivies won't protect their users from flying sticks and chunks of hail like tents or tarps might.

Bivies are the right choice for the person who wants to travel fast and light, is careful to camp under tree cover during heavy rains, doesn't mind stashing gear and doing camp chores outside the shelter, and isn't bothered by small enclosures. For those who like to be on their feet from dawn to dark and who have a fast camp routine of a quick meal and then bed, a bivy might be a strong candidate. A simple, small tarp is often a good companion to a bivy to allow some temporary shelter for meals and camp chores.

Hammock

If you've looked at tents, tarps, and bivies and aren't convinced that they fit your style, you might want to think about a hammock.

Of all shelter types, the hammock has quite possibly the most passionate set of followers. Many a hammock user, upon being posed the question "How do you like your hammock?" is likely to talk your ear off about how the hammock is the best thing to grace backpacking since lime chili shrimp ramen. Why could this be? Based on feedback about hammocks

> Of survey respondents who were AT finishers, 22 percent reported using a hammock. At 2 percent, the hammock was far less popular amongst PCT finishers.

on the 2011 survey, this may be because hammocks get big kudos for being comfortable, especially for those who have not gotten comfortable sleeping on the ground. Below are the responses to the question "What did you like the most about your shelter?":

- Comfort.
- So comfortable! I had a hard time sleeping on the ground.
- Comfort and a variety of terrain to set up.
- Small, light, quick to put up, not muddy in the morning.
- Fast and easy to set up.
- Not sleeping on the ground.
- Comfortable.

Hammock dislikes were a little more diverse:

- Occasionally had to sleep on the ground with it due to complete lack of trees/posts.
- If I slept at high elevation or in fog, condensation would collect on the inside.
- Not being able to camp in towns as easily.
- No privacy, too small rain fly.
- Bugs got in.
- Slightly heavier than some minimalist tents.
- Cold on windy days.

The obvious difference between hammocks and all other shelter types is that hammocks can be slung between two tall objects and suspended in the air. However, hammocks can also be pitched on the ground, where they act like a bivy sack with a rain fly. This makes hammocks highly versatile. Compare and contrast the ground-pitched hammock with other ground-based shelters: An ultralight hammock pitched on the ground is similar in weight and cost to using a simple bivy with an 8 by 10-inch silnylon tarp. While the lightest tarp tents tend to be lighter and less expensive than a hammock, tarp tents are usually single-wall designs and may not be as weatherproof as a ground-pitched hammock with a rain fly. One-person, traditional tents with a rain fly tend to be roomier, but heavier than a hammock. So even if you don't intended to sleep up in the air, the hammock may still be a sound choice.

Shopping for a hammock is pretty straightforward as there are only a few manufacturers and you won't be bogged down comparing specifications and technology. With hammocks, the less weight you want to carry, the more you're going to spend. A few things, then, to consider before purchasing a hammock:

Staking for ground use. If you want to use a hammock on the ground, the hammock will require some sort of staking as it's not a freestanding structure. You'll need a ground pad to insulate and cushion your body from the ground. Pitching on a bare, rocky, treeless slope or under windy conditions will be difficult.

Try before you buy. Most hammock users intend to sleep off the ground. Because slowly swinging back and forth off the ground is a fairly novel way of sleeping, try out a hammock before you buy one. Not everyone likes to be suspended in the air in a sling at night. Big box outdoor retailers are unlikely to have a backpacking hammock on display, which limits tryout to outdoor shows and hiker conferences, where you can usually find hammock vendors. These days, however, many online retailers have generous return policies, so you may be able to order a hammock online and returned it used for an exchange or refund.

Skill to set up. Properly lashing a hammock between trees or other objects requires some skill. You'll need to dedicate some time to practice and learn how to lash quickly and efficiently before you head out on the trail or else risk fumbling and cursing on a dark, cold, rainy night.

Not for couples. As of this writing, there isn't a two-person hammock being sold. There are obvious personal space complications involved with putting two people in a hammock. Couples, even if you're madly in love, seek the tent or tarp tent for weight, space, cost, and relationship savings. **Weight limit.** Big folks be aware: hammocks have weight limits.

Sleeping Bag

Sleeping bags are another piece of essential gear for which there are many choices with a dizzying number of variables. Enough can't be said about having a warm, comfortable sleeping bag, so finding the right kind of bag is well worth the time you take to do the research.

To get past the confusion of so many technological variables, it's helpful to have a decision-making rubric to follow in order to narrow down the choices.

1. Decide on cost. What's your budget?
2. Decide on fill. Are you going with synthetic or down?
3. Decide on temperature rating. How cold do you expect the weather to be where you're going? Are you a cold or warm sleeper?
4. Do your research and try out a few models.
5. Choose a ground pad.

A number of sleeping systems, such as the wearable quilt, are different from sleeping bags and will not be addressed here. If you are interested in alternate sleep systems, by all means check them out. There are a number of hiker blogs and lightweight backpacking sites full of good information and reviews. Keep in mind, however, that most other sleeping systems are sold by small manufacturers, and it's unlikely that you'll be able to try before you buy unless you encounter one on a trail or attend an outdoor show or hiker's conference. Make sure that whatever sleep system you choose, the manufacturer has a good return policy.

Cost

There are few types of gear where the old adage "You get what you pay for" holds true. Sleeping bags are one of them. An ultralight, highly compressible down bag with high fill power made with a name-brand water-repellant fabric with a generous warranty or return policy (all good features) will cost a pretty penny. On the up side, most well-made bags will last for many, many long trips if properly cared for.

Having said this, you don't need to go out and buy the most expensive sleeping bag on the market. If you're a first timer, see if you enjoy long-distance hiking before you go out and spend tons of money on a sleeping bag. Plenty of successful long-distance hikes have been completed with budget bags. However, you sacrifice some nice features to lower cost. If you're on a budget, you must decide what features you absolutely need and which ones you can live without. If you're not on a budget and are expecting to make a lifetime hobby out of distance hiking, then by all means go for a more expensive model. Expect to pay around $400 for a high-end three-season bag.

> "Fill power" is a technical term describing the quality of down in a garment or sleeping bag. A higher number indicates that there is more loft, or trapped air in the insulation, and thus the garment is more efficient at insulating its user. Comparing two identical bags with the same temperature rating, the bag with the higher fill power weighs less.

Another way to save money when shopping for sleeping bags is to look for minimal features. Things like full-length zippers, padloops, and stash pockets aren't critical to a bag's performance. Finally, look for a used bag. Although you risk getting a bag that has been damaged, a savvy shopper can get a good deal.

Fill

There are two basic types of insulating fill for sleeping bags: synthetic and goose down. Although the quality of synthetic fibers has improved substantially over the years, a bag filled with down will usually be lighter and more compressible than a bag of the same temperature rating filled with a synthetic material. The advantage of synthetic fill is that it is less expensive than down and performs much better when wet. Synthetic fill

> Personally, I'm willing to give a little on fancy water-repellent fabrics and less likely to sacrifice on fill, weight, manufacturer reputation, and compressibility.

also dries faster. Down clumps and is basically useless when wet. Thus, when making a decision about fill, think about how wet the climate is where you'll be traveling. Trails in the eastern United States tend to be wetter than those out West. This means that not only are you likely to experience more rain, but things will also take much longer to dry. Some hikers feel that, under these circumstances, choosing synthetic is worth the extra weight and bulk.

If you decide to go with down and are hiking in a wet climate, you will need to take extra care to keep your bag dry by using a good pack cover, being careful about keeping it dry when it's out of your pack, and/or enclosing it inside an additional barrier like a garbage bag to keep it separate from wet things in your pack. You might also want to choose a bag made from a fabric with good water-repellant qualities, although this will significantly increase the bag's cost. Finally, when traveling in a wet climate with a down bag, consider what shelter you'll be in. Will you be in a tent or other enclosed shelter that is unlikely to let in the rain, or will you be under a tarp or something with open edges that might let water blow or soak in during a windy deluge?

Temperature rating

Once you've decided on either down or synthetic, the next thing to choose is the temperature rating. Temperature rating refers to the outside air temperature limit where a person feels comfortable inside a sleeping bag. A bag rated at +30 degrees F is supposed to be comfortable to sleep in when the air temperature is above 30 degrees. Use caution when interpreting temperature ratings, though, because they are not exact figures.

One reason ratings are inexact is that many are specific to the manufacturer, meaning that a bag rated at +30 degrees F from manufacturer X may act like a +20-degree bag from manufacturer Y. While this might seem to make any meaningful comparison impossible, the good news is that a universal standard for bag ratings has been developed. In fact, it

Most EN13537-rated bags have three ratings:

Comfort: The lowest air temperature where an average woman would still feel comfortable.

Lower limit: The lowest air temperature where an average man would still feel comfortable.

Extreme: Survival air temperature for a woman. Not really helpful for backpacking applications.

has been widely adopted by European manufacturers, and a handful of American manufacturers are now using it. This rating system, known as EN13537, was developed in 2002 and uses a heated manikin in an independent lab to create temperature numbers that describe how the bag performs in various conditions. Since the process is standardized and not manufacturer specific, bags labeled with the EN13537 rating are easier to compare.

Despite the growing acceptance of the EN13537 rating system among bag manufacturers, temperature ratings are still inexact and will continue to be so even if the entire worldwide industry were to accept the EN13537 standard for the simple reason that people come in different sizes, shapes, and body compositions and don't feel universally cold or hot under the same conditions. Even a particular person may feel warmer or colder under the same temperature conditions depending on calorie intake for the day and whether the person is going to sleep wet, damp, or dry. The EN13537 standard is only able to deduce how a standard 176-pound man or standard 132-pound woman *might* feel at certain temperature levels. Despite temperature rating, some people require more insulation to feel warm at 30 degrees and some people require less.

The graph shows the range of sleeping bag temperature ratings carried by thru-hikers on the AT and PCT in 2011. Most hikers carried bags in the range of +10 to +29 degrees.

So why bother with temperature ratings at all? Ratings, though inexact, still help describe the performance expectation for a sleeping bag. In other words, the rating will put you in the right neighborhood and narrow down your options.

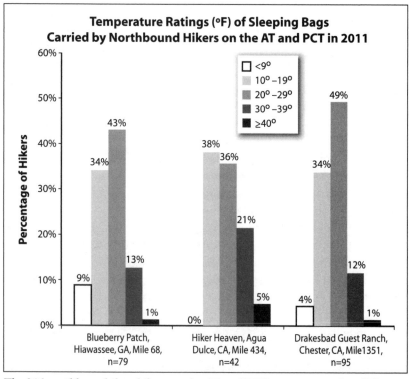

The 216 northbound thru-hikers on the AT and PCT were surveyed at different points along the trail.

Say you're starting the Appalachian Trail from Georgia in mid-April and you're a cold sleeper. The highest shelter on the Georgia AT is Blood Mountain at 4,500 feet. Dahlonega, Georgia (1,430 feet), has an average low temperature in April of 43 degrees. Subtract 9.5 degrees (3.5 degrees x 3 for the 3,000-foot gain in elevation), and you can deduce that you can reasonably expect to encounter temps down to 33 degrees. Since you're a cold sleeper, pack either a +20-degree bag or a +30-degree bag and wear your jacket inside the bag on cold nights.

How do you know what rating to choose? First determine if you are a cold, warm, or average sleeper. Cold sleepers tend to get cold easier. They might start to get uncomfortable in a +30-degree bag when outdoor temperatures are still at 40 degrees above zero. Warm sleepers are just the opposite. They might be able to tolerate temperatures down to 20 degrees above zero in a +30-degree bag. If you're not sure if you're a warm or cold sleeper, think about this: When others are chilly or bundling up, are you still comfy in long sleeves or a T-shirt? If so, you might be a warm sleeper. What if everyone else is happy in a T-shirt and you feel you need a sweater? Then you could be a cold sleeper. If you're usually wearing the same clothing as everyone else, then you're probably average.

If you're a cold sleeper, you can do one or two things when it comes to choosing a temperature rating to make sure you are comfortable. First, pick a bag that is rated 10 degrees lower than the lowest temperature you're reasonably expecting to encounter on your hike. This is the more conservative method and will result in carrying a bit more weight and spending more money for an extra margin of safety. The other technique is to buy a bag with a normal temperature rating and commit to sleeping with a warm jacket on when nights are cold. This technique will save you money (you need to carry a warm jacket anyway) and will lighten your pack.

If you're a warm sleeper, choose a bag 10 degrees warmer than the lowest expected temperature on your hiking trip. You can even perhaps go another 5 degrees higher than this and wear a warm jacket at night like the cold sleeper. I'd be cautious about going too high, though. Warm sleepers might want to pay more attention to a bag's zipper system as well. Hot nights can be unbearable for a warm sleeper, who will appreciate the ability to unzip various portions of the bag for ventilation.

Once you've decided if you sleep warm, cold, or average, find out what the average low temperatures are where you'll be traveling. Be sure to subtract 3.5 degrees for every 1,000 feet gain in elevation.

	Average Low Temperatures (°F) Near Popular U.S. Long-Distance Trailheads												
	Elevation (ft.)	Jan	Feb	Mar	Apr	May	Jun	Jul	Aug	Sept	Oct	Nov	Dec
Dahlonega, GA	1,560	29	30	37	43	52	59	63	64	57	46	37	30
Gage, NM	4,478	28	31	36	43	52	62	67	66	59	47	35	27
Cuyamaca, CA	4,640	31	32	35	36	43	49	58	55	49	40	34	30
Stehekin, WA	1,270	26	26	30	35	42	49	56	55	47	37	30	26
Kalispell, MT	2,957	17	19	25	31	38	44	49	46	39	30	25	17
Millinocket, ME	360	5	8	16	28	38	50	55	54	45	36	28	14

Source: NOAA National Climatic Data Center Asheville, NC. Data is for 10 years spanning 2001–2010.

Research

After deciding on cost, fill material, and temperature rating, your choices should be narrowed down to a few bags. Now is the time to dig in and do some research. Stats and figures can only go so far when shopping for a sleeping bag, so hit the blogs, backpacking websites, and shops to see how other people liked sleeping in the bags you've picked. Keep in mind when reading reviews:

Subjectivity. A reviewer might bash a sleeping bag for not performing in a certain way when, in fact, the reviewer was not using the bag in the way it was intended. A good review will always be specific in listing conditions under which the bag was evaluated. At the minimum, the reviewer should talk about the climate conditions and type of ground pad and shelter used with the sleeping bag as well as how well the reviewer fit inside the bag. It's also helpful to know if the reviewer is a warm, cold, or average sleeper, if the user is near your size, sex, and shape, and if she or he was wet or damp before using the bag.

Conflicts of interest. Even though advertising and editorial departments are often separate, there may be a conflict of interest when an information source that advertises or sells products also reviews them. This is not to say that all sources that sell or advertise gear are giving biased reviews, but read these reviews with a little bit of skepticism and make certain the claims can be backed up by independent reviewers.

Jargon and details. A lot of technology goes into sleeping bag construction, and it's easy to get overwhelmed with minute details like different types of synthetic fibers, styles of baffling, and so forth. As sleeping bag design becomes more and more efficient, manufacturers need to find ways to set themselves apart. In the grand scheme of being a successful distance hiker, the small technological details mean little. Bags within the limits you have set that have consistently good reviews will be your best indicator of quality and comfort.

If you can, go to a store and try out the bag. You want to make sure the bag is a comfortable fit for a quality night's sleep. Some bags are better for wider people, some fit slimmer people better. Most bags for backpacking are mummy-shaped as the mummy is the most thermally efficient type of bag, so get used to the mummy's tight quarters, but make sure there's some wiggle room. A bag that is too tight around the body will compress the insulation and reduce the bag's performance. On the other hand, a bag that is too roomy will leave too much dead air and be thermally inefficient. You should have a few inches to spare at the foot with the thickest part of the bag near the upper chest. If you plan to sleep with a jacket on, bring it to wear inside the bag when you try it.

Sleeping bags usually come in two or three standard sizes: short, regular, and long are the most common labels. These sizes will fit most men and women. However, if you are someone whose height falls far outside the standard sizes, you might need to do a little extra shopping or make some accommodations. Very short people might just need to scoot further down in a short bag or scrunch parts of the bag up. The bigger issue is for very tall people where there isn't enough bag for the person. Some manufacturers sell extra-long bags at little extra cost. The other option for both very short and very tall people where budget isn't an issue is to find a manufacturer (there are a few) who will custom-size a bag.

Ground pad

Lastly, choose a ground pad. Sleeping bags don't stand up to the cold when they are placed directly on the ground. The ground pads most often seen on long-distance trails are either inflatable or closed cell.

The inflatable ground pad is usually carried deflated in or outside the pack during the day. At night, it is unrolled, blown up, and placed under the sleeping bag, giving the hiker a cushion of air between him or her and the ground. The major advantage of the inflatable pad is that it is a bit more comfortable to sleep on than closed-cell foam.

Closed-cell foam does not inflate or deflate, so you are more apt

An excellent way to save weight is to choose a short pad instead of one that is full-length. If you need to have your feet off the ground at night, prop them up on your pack (emptied of food, of course) or some extra clothes.

to feel what lies underneath the pad at night. There are, however, a number of advantages of using closed-cell foam. One advantage is in the ease of deployment. Closed-cell foam can provide a quick, comfy place to sit during breaks, and some can be draped to conform to objects like logs and rocks. This is more difficult with an inflatable pad, which is more rigid and takes time to inflate. Closed-cell pads are also not prone to malfunctioning. A poorly handled inflatable pad may puncture. Closed-cell foam typically costs less. Some hikers believe you can address the problems associated with a less comfortable sleep on closed-cell foam by choosing soft areas, such as pine needle beds, to sleep in. Understandably, though, soft areas are not always available.

> I usually find that if I happen to roll off my ground pad and become cold, I wake up and readjust. It's not a big deal for me. For some hikers, it may be more important.

Some sleeping bag manufacturers integrate their bags with proprietary sleeping pads, physically mating the two with a sleeve or straps. The claims are that physically coupling the pad with the bag is the most thermally efficient method and eliminates problems of rolling off the ground pad. Weight savings are also suggested. With the right products, some of these claims may be true. However, you may lose some versatility when choosing a bag that can only conform to a pad by the same manufacturer.

4

Resupply

On the PCT in 2007 I resupplied in every way imaginable, from standard shipped-ahead mail drops to the time-refined art of the yogi (thru-hiker slang for begging food off other hikers and tourists). In California and southern Oregon, I combined bounce boxes with local shopping. Into the box went things that I could buy ahead of time in large quantities that might be hard to find in a town without a supermarket: powdered milk, Carnation Instant Breakfast, rolls of gauze, first-aid supplies, medication, device chargers, denatured alcohol, extra batteries, favorite foods and candy, extra paper and pens, and so on. Locally, I'd pick up easy-to-find stuff like mac and cheese and candy bars to complete my resupply. As long as I didn't arrive in town on Friday after post office hours, this system worked out pretty well, even in the High Sierra, where getting to a post office meant taking a side trail to a road leading 20 or more miles to town.

> A bounce box is a box full of supplies that are needed frequently, but don't need to be carried every day. The box gets "bounced" along the trail by being shipped ahead one or several resupply points at a time.

> If you label and package denatured alcohol properly, the U.S. Postal Service will ship it. Most canister fuel cannot be shipped.

By central Oregon I had become a fairly fast but stubborn and self-sufficient hiker. I was hiking at a pace of 27 to 30 miles per day, and the idea of a resupply itinerary limited by post office hours no longer appealed to me. So at Crater Lake National Park, I said goodbye to the bounce box for a while and decided to wing it and make my way through central and northern Oregon resupplying with whatever was available locally. I sent medication to a cousin's house in Hood River, Oregon, and made sure to carry enough with me to last. I ditched my alcohol stove for a wood-burning stove so I didn't need to worry about carrying or finding fuel in towns.

This strategy worked pretty well. Central and northern Oregon are dotted by small campgrounds, most of which have stores that are a brief walk off the trail. Although the variety of food I was able to carry was limited to what the stores stocked, I was usually able to get a good selection, aided by the ubiquitous presence of "hiker boxes," unadvertised supplies of random junk that many trailside stores keep. Hikers who oversupply or want to lighten their loads contribute to the hiker box. It's the backpacking equivalent of take a penny, leave a penny. On northern Oregon's Mt. Hood, where the store didn't have much food, I relied exclusively on the hiker box in the gift shop and ended up with random concoctions of dehydrated soups and meals plus energy bars to take me the last miles to the Washington border. I benefitted from being a bit ahead of the pack that year, so I had a good selection. I might not have been so confident about hiker boxes had I been late in the season.

In Washington, I had to adopt another strategy, mainly because my hiking style had evolved to making as few stops as possible. I wanted to experience Washington, my last state, with as few town distractions as possible. This meant either depending on the convenience stores at White Pass and Snoqualmie Pass (the only resupply points within reasonable walking distance of the trail) for all my supplies or buying all my food ahead of time in Cascade Locks, the last town stop in Oregon, and shipping it ahead. I chose the latter option, shipping two boxes of food and supplies to the convenience store at White Pass and the motel at Snoqualmie Pass. While I never stepped into a car in the whole state of Washington, I did end up undersupplying and was forced to yogi my way through the last days on the trail in northern Washington (see pages 1 to 3).

One of the most frequent questions I get about the PCT is how to resupply along the trail. I usually refer folks to guidebooks that lay out what's in the trail towns so they get a sense, for planning purposes, of what will be available and what won't. What I've found in practice, however, is that resupplying depends on a person's hiking style, which will change along the course of a long-distance trail. I've known folks who plan mail drops ahead of time from terminus to terminus, only to quickly abandon their itinerary once on the trail and just plan as they go (to the chagrin of loved ones at home). If this is your first hike and you don't yet have a good sense of your pace and style, it's probably easiest to send along a bounce box to a post office and combine this with local purchases as I did on much of the PCT. You can usually fit essentials and hard-to-find items in a single medium- or large-sized flat-rate box to keep shipping costs at a predictable level.

The next few sections in this chapter will discuss different ways of re-supplying along long-distance trails in the United States. Hopefully these will help you make more informed choices that fit your own style.

Mail drops/bounce box

In a mail drop, food and supplies are shipped either to a post office facility or other location willing to accept hiker packages, such as hiker hostels, gas stations, motels, or campgrounds. While the post office holds packages for free, many other locations charge a fee to hikers as packages take up space and sometimes must be transported long distances. Packages going through post offices must be labeled to notify the post office staff that the package should be held for pickup at the post office. They should include all of the following:

> In California's High Sierra, trail-convenient Muir Trail Ranch charges $55 to hold hiker buckets up to 25 pounds. Cost is $2 a pound thereafter (2011 pricing). This may seem unreasonable, but consider that to transport buckets, the ranch has to drive them 24 miles from the post office and then transport them to the ranch by horse or special rock-crawling truck. The ranch also handles trash and must deal with unclaimed buckets. The alternative is to hike half a day to an entire day (each way) to a road and hitch into a town.

General Delivery
Town, State, ZIP
Please hold for hiker (insert full name), expected on (insert date)

The United States Postal Service (USPS) will hold a package for no longer than 30 days. Mail drops are useful for ensuring a reliable supply of everything you want. If there's a specific blend of food you absolutely must have or if a loved one insists on keeping you fed from home, it makes sense to have a mail drop.

> Because bounce boxes get so much handling, they should be made of strong material or well reinforced. This saves money in purchasing new boxes and ensures your box won't fall apart in the mail.

A bounce box is a type of mail drop that is forwarded up the trail by the hiker. The bounce box allows you to buy in bulk without having to carry the entire amount in a backpack.

This is not necessarily a way to save money, as the cost advantage of buying in bulk is probably negated by the cost of shipping up the trail.

Buying in town

If you choose to rely on town purchase for resupply, you will obviously be at the mercy of whatever might be available. In some cases, you might be resupplying for 100 miles or more out of a gas station convenience store. In others, you might have entire supermarkets at your disposal. Plan ahead if you're going to rely exclusively on town purchases. A good strategy is to combine town purchases with a bounce box.

Certain sections of trails sometimes run quite close to local campgrounds, which can contain small stores and hiker boxes. The Oregon section of the PCT is a good example. However, don't assume that because a campground is close by that it contains a well-stocked general store. In fact, don't assume that a campground has any type of store at all. You will be greatly disappointed when, instead of a store, you encounter a water spigot, a picnic table, and some grass. Sometimes you're lucky to get any of these. Also be aware of campground store hours, which frequently change, are seasonal, and tend to be short. Calling ahead from the prior resupply point is a good idea.

> For more information on resupply options in trail towns near the AT, PCT, and CDT, there are a few noteworthy publications. For the AT, try using the *ALDHA Guide*. Yogi's *PCT Handbook* and *CDT Handbook* provide this kind of detail for their respective trails.

Other methods

You can often find communal free supplies called hiker boxes at hostels, post offices, or at any other town establishment friendly to hikers. They are filled by hikers who may have overstocked on an item or by members of the local community who are friendly to hikers. The boxes are quite common along the AT and PCT, less so along other trails. Savvy long-distance hikers often check the hiker boxes first before purchasing supplies. Hiker boxes usually aren't a resupply strategy by themselves. They're more of a way to save money and add variety to an existing resupply strategy.

You can also yogi food from other hikers and tourists. The yogi cannot realistically be counted upon as a primary resupply strategy, but it's reliable for netting a few extra calories during summer months when traveling through popular parks, especially on weekends. I elected to use the yogi to get to Canada in 2007.

The ability to appear hungry and despondent is helpful for a successful yogi. My friends Optimist and Stopwatch, who have the ability to look like they've fasted with Ghandi after being dragged through a garbage dump, repeatedly gain the horror-stricken sympathy of passersby, who insist on inviting them to cookouts and putting them up for the night. Optimist and Stopwatch happen to be fantastic company, so this is always a mutually beneficial arrangement.

5

Repetitive Stress Injury

When the Brain Gets Ahead of the Body

An injury nearly put an early end to my southbound Appalachian Trail (AT) thru-hike in 2002. Rejoining the trail in Monson, Maine, after some time off, I was anxious to catch up to friends I had made along the 100-mile wilderness, the AT's most remote section of trail just south of its Katahdin terminus. To make up for lost ground, I started hiking 20-plus-mile days, a large increase from the 15 to 20 daily miles I was accustomed to prior to my time away. After about a week at this pace, carrying 40 to 50 pounds of pack weight, my right knee began to hurt terribly. It was a sharp, gripping pain around my kneecap. The pain was at its worst on the hills, particularly when walking downhill. It intensified as I plodded on through Maine's steep mountain terrain, picking my way gingerly over the rocks and roots. As I approached where the trail crossed a state highway, it looked like I was going to have to take more time off as the pain had gotten so bad I could no longer bear to walk downhill forward. Each time I encountered a downhill section, I turned around and walked backward so my knee wouldn't hurt. I probably walked the last eight miles to Route 4 in reverse. Limping out onto the road, I hitched into the town of Rangeley and located the nearest pay phone. I returned home for a few days to recover, and when I returned to the trail, I had armed myself with trekking poles, a neoprene knee sleeve, and had begun taking ibuprofen. After several weeks of careful hiking at reduced mileage and relying heavily on the poles for the downhill hiking, as well as making major changes to my load to reduce pack weight, the pain in my knees went away and I started tapering my ibuprofen intake. By the time I reached Vermont, the pain had completely gone away, but I continued using the poles until I got to northern Virginia.

The injury to my knee was caused by hiking too aggressively through Maine too soon into the trail and with more weight than my body could adapt to quickly. As a result, my knee, which bore a large chunk of the physical strain, became irritated and painful, forcing me off the trail. Had I been smart about pack weight (it was my first-ever solo backpacking trip) and kept my mileage at lower levels during my first few weeks through Maine, I may have avoided injury entirely.

Injury plagues the majority of thru-hikers at some point in the journey. In fact, injury is one of the more popular reasons why people leave the trail. The graph shows that of the 32 hikers who completed the 2011 survey but did not finish the trail, injury was cited as influential by 25 percent.

Of the 85 thru-hikers who completed the 2011 survey and finished the trail, an impressive 83.5 percent reported experiencing a bodily injury or

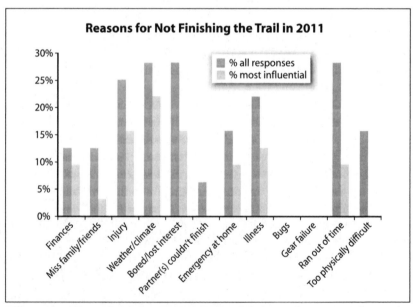

Hikers who did not finish the AT or PCT listed their top three most influential reasons for leaving the trail. Thirty-two hikers listed a total of 62 responses. The darker bars indicate the percentage of hikers who chose each category as their first, second, or third most influential reason for leaving the trail. The lighter bars indicate the percentage of hikers who chose each category as their most influential reason for leaving the trail.

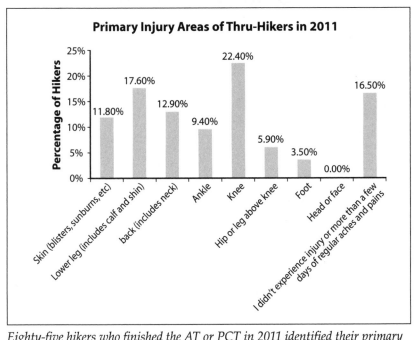

Eighty-five hikers who finished the AT or PCT in 2011 identified their primary injury area.

more than a few days of regular aches and pains along the way. Not surprisingly, feet and knee injuries were the most common.

Judging by their responses, posted at the end of this chapter, many injuries seemed to be repetitive stress injuries.

The Anatomy of a Repetitive Stress Injury

A repetitive stress injury occurs when a body structure becomes injured from being used in a way it is not accustomed to. This may be due to an unexpected magnitude of force, an unusual frequency of use, an unusual duration of use, an unusual mode of use, or a combination of all four.

To understand how body parts become injured by repetitive stress, it's helpful to understand how the body responds to regular stress. Many structures in the body require a normal window of stress to stay healthy. For instance, the Achilles tendon, which attaches the calf muscles to the heel, requires the everyday stress and strain of walking to maintain a functional level of tensile strength and elasticity so it can continue to do its job. If a person stops walking for a long period of time, the tendon will become weaker and if the person tries to suddenly resume walking at their usual level, they may experience difficulty and risk injury. On the other hand, a person who needs to use his Achilles tendon at higher forces can, with proper training, cause it to adapt and become more able to handle these high forces. A runner training for a marathon might go through such an adaptive process. Indeed, the Achilles tendon of runners has been estimated to handle peak loads of 6.1 to 8.2 times body weight.

> My trail name is Achilles, a name I acquired not through brave acts, but through an injured Achilles tendon that I couldn't stop complaining about!

At the cell level, this process of adaptation is characterized by damage and repair. An excessively stressed body part will initially experience microtrauma, or small tears in connective tissue and cell damage. With sufficient rest, the body can repair the microtrauma and become stronger in anticipation of responding to the same stresses again. The key to this adaptive response is rest. The body requires a period of reduced intensity to allow overstressed structures to repair.

Injury occurs when the same excessive stresses happen over and over again without sufficient rest. As a result, microtrauma is inadequately repaired, becoming cumulative and causing maladaptations like abnormal collagen (connective tissue) formation, abnormal vascular (blood vessel) growth, hypoxia (lack of oxygen), and the accumulation of cells called myofibroblasts, which do not normally exist in large numbers in healthy body structures. The body structure, now injured, will eventually become painful and will continue to be painful until proper treatment is applied.

Long-distance hikers are at high risk for repetitive stress injuries. Most of us come straight from so-called civilized life, where everyday walking occurs over level terrain without the weight of a backpack and with plenty of rest in the form of sitting. Instantly transform us tender-footed citizens into long-distance hikers, who tromp 20-plus miles over variable terrain with a backpack, and what happens? The body parts responsible for handling the bulk of the forces of everyday walking (knees and feet) are suddenly working overtime and handling significantly increased forces without adequate rest. It's a recipe for a repetitive stress injury.

Injuries aren't pleasant, and hiking with constant pain can be a miserable experience. Although some pain and discomfort is probably inevitable due to the extreme nature of long-distance hiking, being equipped to both minimize risk and manage repetitive stress injuries on the trail can lead to a more positive experience.

The first half of this chapter reviews preventive methods that will minimize the risk of sustaining a repetitive stress injury during a long-distance hike. Many of these methods follow the common-sense philosophy of reducing sudden, excessive loading and gradually introducing the body to its new role of long-distance hiker. These concepts are introduced here in an easy-to-understand, nontechnical manner. The second half of the chapter discusses some ways of managing repetitive stress injuries on the trail before they get worse and cause the unthinkable—the end to a hike.

Prevention

Injury prevention is one of the biggest topics in this book—and rightfully so. There are so many things that hikers can do both prior to a hike and while on the trail to ensure that the body is given its best chance to adapt to the stresses of distance hiking without injury. There are many more ways of preventing injuries than are listed in this chapter. However, these topics are the most important and not only cover a lot of diverse ground, but also reinforce some basic principles. These principles are the key to injury prevention in backpacking, and if you can remember these, you'll do well.

1. *Ease into it.* The body will grow stronger and will mostly do as you wish if you allow it time to adapt.
2. *Prepare.* Take a little time to get your body ready for what you're about to ask it to do. This includes preparation up to the start day of the hike and doing a little something each day while on the trail.
3. *Make sure things fit and are comfortable.* Fit and comfort are related, but not exactly the same. Whatever goes on your body should be a good fit in order to avoid problems like chafing and blisters. This chapter will describe some fit guidelines for important choices like shoes and backpacks. Something that fits should also be comfortable, meaning that it feels good on your body. If it feels good, you will be less likely to try and do something with your body to move away from it. If a tag on a shirt is bothering you, cut it off. If a fabric just doesn't feel right, pick a different garment.
4. *Get to know yourself.* This means taking a hard look at your physical and mental condition and knowing where things might go wrong. Do you have a past injury that might act up? How do you handle

pain, fatigue, stress, and other physical discomforts? Things that don't affect you in everyday life might start to do so on the trail. Now on to the specifics.

Pack weight

The subject of lightweight backpacking is discussed ad nauseum in the long-distance hiking community. Most long-distance hikers are quite proud of surviving on less stuff, and ultralighters, who carry 10 pounds or less of base weight, are usually happy to show off their thimble-sized stoves, handmade gear, sawed-off toothbrushes, and no-frills backpacks. The ultralighters have the right idea in that, simply put, a lighter pack means less stress and strain on the body and potentially a lower risk of injury. Does this mean that carrying under 10 pounds of base weight is the only way to avoid injury?

> Base weight is the weight of a pack loaded with gear, but without food and water.

Being able to reduce pack weight is certainly a step in the right direction, but you don't need to be an ultralighter to cut down on injury risk. Plenty of successful long-distance hikers carry heavier loads simply because it's what they're comfortable with. In my experience, there is a reasonable range of base weights that will lower the risk of suffering a repetitive stress injury on the trail.

> My wife and I once met a man thru-hiking the Continental Divide Trail (CDT) northbound in southwestern Montana. He was carrying 78 pounds in his pack and told us that he enjoyed the many comforts of its contents. He had no qualms about the weight. Since he had successfully walked over 2,000 miles of trail in a single season, his body had clearly adapted to the heavy pack. He was, however, late in the season and well behind the group. We wondered if he was going to make it up to Canada before the snow.

Assuming an adequate, but not excessive, supply of calorie-dense food (see chapter 1 on diet), base weights under 20 pounds will provide good risk reduction and still permit comfortable five- to six-day excursions between resupply points. Hikers who can get their base weights down to 10 to 15 pounds may realize an even greater risk reduction. Keep in mind, however, that pack weight is just one piece of the injury risk puzzle and, interestingly, the few scientific studies that have looked at pack weight and musculoskeletal injury have failed to find a significant relationship. It's not helpful to be myopic about pack weight and ignore the other equally important aspects of reducing risk of injury, like gradually increasing your mileage and having good footwear.

Those who carry base weights over 20 pounds can still successfully complete a long-distance hike, but risk of injury might be higher and the going will probably be slower.

If you're not sure about how to cut down your base pack weight, books on lightweight backpacking are widely available. Veteran and novice long-distance hikers alike will benefit from reading any of these for some ideas on pack weight reduction. The other places to go for ideas are online hiker bulletin boards like whiteblaze.net, a community of Appalachian Trail enthusiasts, or the PCT-L, the Pacific Crest Trail list. Just post a list of your gear and ask for help trimming it down, and then sit back and watch all the replies come in.

Another good place to start in keeping pack weight down is to use a low- to mid-volume pack. For three-season long-distance hiking in the United States, packs that hold between 3,000 and 4,000 cubic inches in volume are ideally sized for my style. Going for higher volumes might add a greater feeling of security, but they may result in the temptation to carry too much gear. Higher volume packs may also weigh more, as materials need to be stronger and structural supports added to make carrying the high-volume load comfortable.

Go to a reputable outfitter to get started learning about backpacks. Seek out someone on staff who has experience with long-distance hiking (this might not be the person in the backpacks section). This person will understand the need to carry a well-made pack that has a reasonable volume for a low weight and price. She may secretly disclose to you that the kind of pack you're looking for isn't sold in the store and can only be found online. Now that's honest

> Try to choose an outfitter that specializes in outdoor adventure travel rather than one that generalizes in everything outdoors. You'll get a higher quality selection as well as more knowledgeable staff.

customer service! If this is the case, you'll still want to try on a few packs to get a sense of what sizes and shapes suit you best. Be skeptical of the salesperson who, upon hearing about your long-distance itinerary, steers you toward the biggest, heaviest packs on the shelf. He is either not likely to have any personal experience with long-distance hiking or is under a lot of pressure to sell a certain product. Either way, your best interests are not being considered.

One final note about pack shopping: Don't pay attention to manufacturer's descriptions of what constitutes "long haul" versus "medium haul" packs. While stores and manufacturers may use different terms to describe these categories, they are all exclusively based on pack volume. They assume that hikers on longer trips need to pile more stuff in their packs. This formula does not consider the individual needs and creative powers of long-distance hikers. While all long-distance hikers are out for the "long haul," not everyone needs a high-volume pack. A good pack for long-distance hiking is one that can carry your things comfortably, has a good reputation for durability, is light-weight, and is priced right. Also take a critical look at a pack's accessories. Strategically placed zippers, ice axe loops, and stash pockets are handy, but add weight, complexity, and price. Can you organize your things without having a ton of pockets? Probably so.

> My own preference is a few stretchy stash pockets and a single main pack with a drawstring. I like to have good padding on the belt and back, but I don't need fancy pack frames.

Pack fit

In addition to maintaining a low base pack weight, pay attention to the fit of a pack. A poorly fitting pack may put abnormal stress and strain on parts of the body such as the neck, shoulders, and spine and could lead to a constantly uncomfortable hike, creating the potential for repetitive stress injury. There are some fairly straightforward guidelines when it comes to achieving a proper pack fit, but there are also other things to consider.

Basic pack fitting guidelines dictate that the main belt of the pack fit snugly around the iliac crests, those two pointy bony prominences a few inches below and to either side of the belly button. The body of the pack should come no higher than the base of the skull. The chest strap should fit snugly, and the shoulder straps should not be excessively tight or rub. Since backpacks are often designed to carry a certain range of weight and volume, it's important to have an idea of how much volume and weight you intend to carry. Overloading a pack with more stuff than it was intended to carry will compromise the pack's structure and make it uncomfortable to wear. Try on a pack with the things you intend to put in it and see how it feels.

Basic pack fitting guidelines are an important starting point, but beyond these, the fit of a backpack is highly subjective and relies on a person's ability to adapt and adjust. I remember once meeting a long-distance hiker named Roni on the PCT in 2007. I bumped into Roni hanging out under a giant rock with some other hikers on the north slopes of the San Jacinto Mountains in California. He and his companions were preparing

 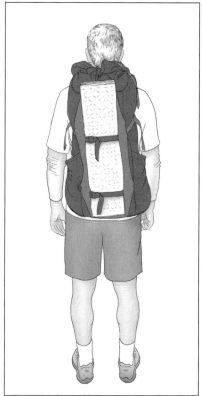

A well-fitting backpack sits high on the hips and allows plenty of room for your head to move. Straps should be snug but comfortable.

to hike across San Gorgonio Pass and ascend into the San Bernardinos. What I noticed about Roni was that he was carrying the most awkward and uncomfortable-looking backpack I'd ever seen a long-distance hiker wear. The pack was huge and seemed to defy all traditional pack fit guidelines. The bottom hung low and well below Roni's waist while the top towered above his head. I couldn't discern the make or model of Roni's pack, as it looked like Roni had either worn the labels off or stitched it himself. The pack seemed to have no intrinsic support or structure, and the whole thing flopped over to the right, giving the impression of a giant gray banana. Roni's sleeping bag was stuffed into a pouch at the rear of his pack, but he had not done a good job at stuffing it all the way in, so it just flopped about with the rest of his pack. Pots and water bottles clanged and dangled on the outside. Sixty-four miles down the trail, I ran into Roni in Big Bear City, hanging around in front of the Kmart scarfing down a large cheese pizza. Here I found out that that Roni was in the midst of his second thru-hike of the PCT, having completed his first several years back. I also learned that Roni is one of the small group of long-distance hikers to have completed the triple crown, a successful completion of the Appalachian, Pacific Crest, and Continental Divide Trails.

Roni's unusual example illustrates that while following good basic guidelines for pack fit might be a way to reduce injury and discomfort, the subjective qualities of pack fit are also important. This is because people come in all different sizes, shapes, and styles, not always fitting neatly into traditional guidelines for pack fitting or commonly available sizes for backpacks. Roni had developed a style and fit that worked for him, probably through trying many different combinations of packing and constantly making adjustments. This is a critical skill for any successful long-distance hiker. Don't throw your arms up in disgust when that perfect-fitting pack at the outfitter is, at first, miserable to carry on the trail. All long-distance hikers make ongoing pack adjustments during a hike, sometimes with funny-looking results.

Mileage

As I hope my story at the beginning of this chapter conveyed, hiking too far too fast at the start of a long-distance trail is a setup for injury. How many daily miles are too many? On the major long-distance trails in the United States, most long-distance hikers are eventually able to walk 20-plus miles per day without much extra effort or undue risk of injury. My own comfortable mileage level was 27 miles per day on the PCT at age 30 and 23 miles per day on the considerably steeper AT at age 25.

Eighty-five hikers filled out surveys at mile 68 on the AT in 2011. The most common daily mileage range was 10 to 14, reported by 60 hikers.

Few people start out at this type of mileage. Those who do are either highly experienced or have done some considerable training. See the graphs for the average daily mileage that a sample of PCT hikers in 2011 reported at mile 454 and at mile 1,351. Trail conditions at both mile points are similar, but hikers covered considerably more daily distance at mile 1,351 than at mile 454. Working up to a high daily mileage takes time. Even after 454 miles (approximately one month) on the trail, PCT hikers were still building their endurance.

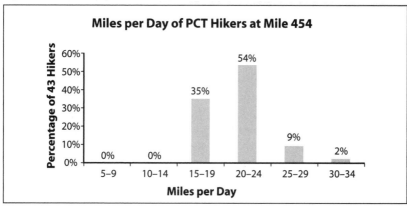

Forty-three PCT thru-hikers reported their daily mileage at Hiker Heaven in Agua Dulce, California.

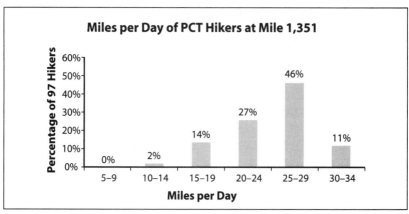

Ninety-seven PCT thru-hikers reported their daily mileage at Drakesbad Guest Ranch in Chester, California.

When starting a long-distance trail, a daily mileage range somewhere between 8 and 15 miles per day is appropriate for most people. The exact mileage varies with age, health and fitness levels, pack weight, experience, and terrain. Younger, fitter people carrying light packs can start at the higher range in comparison to older, less fit people, or those carrying heavy loads. When starting on rocky, steep terrain, it's best to keep mileage at the lower end of the range. There is also some credibility to the notion of muscle memory. That is, hikers with experience making long trips will probably be able to start at higher mileage than those who have no prior experience.

Perhaps just as important as starting daily mileage is the rate at which mileage is increased. You might find yourself in a situation where you fall behind friends and want to quickly up your mileage in an attempt to catch up. Be careful—fit, athletic hikers are just as prone to sustaining repetitive stress injuries as novice hikers when it comes to increasing daily mileage too quickly. On a long-distance trail, just as in everyday life, the body tries its best to shape itself to what it perceives as regular routine. If a hiker has been hiking 25 miles per day and suddenly ups this number to 30-plus, risk of injury may increase.

There's no formula for determining when and how to increase daily mileage. At the start of a trail, staying at the starting daily mileage for a week or two allows the body to grow accustomed to hiking. From there, increasing mileage at a rate of two or three miles per week is easier on the body than an increase of five or six miles. These are general guidelines, and some hikers may want to hike at the starting daily mileage for more than two weeks, some for less. Long-distance trails go on for thousands of miles, and there's plenty of time to catch up to friends.

Trekking poles

Poles are nearly ubiquitous on long-distance trails and can be an easy way to ease the body into hiking. While I personally do not use poles, most people do and generally for good reasons. Poles reduce the burden on the knees and feet by adding two more points of force transfer with the ground. They also aid in balance

Of the 85 thru-hikers who finished a trail in 2011 and took this survey, 91 percent (77 hikers) carried trekking poles.

over difficult terrain and can be a helpful tool in snow or slippery conditions. Some folks rely on poles to set up their shelters at night, making them a good multipurpose piece of gear.

Take caution when using poles for body support. Relying heavily on poles might not give the body its best chance to adapt to its new daily hiking routine, since some of the additional force is being transferred through poles rather than the body. I do not use poles because I believe that if I pay attention to keeping a low pack weight, have good footwear, and am cautious with mileage, my body will effectively adapt to the trail. I also don't like having things in my hands when I hike. However, many people wisely use poles for injury prevention, and my choice is one more of personal philosophy than scientific merit. If you're on the fence about poles, try taking them along and using them only when terrain is difficult or when your legs are tired. If they seem to be helpful, keep them. If not, send them home.

Footwear

Supportive, comfortable, and well-fitting footwear will reduce the risk of injury throughout your body. Poorly fitting footwear alters biomechanical stresses at the foot and

Boots worn over long distances are often associated with foot problems. The 2011 thru-hiker survey identified only 9 (out of 85) thru-hikers who finished the trail wearing boots most of the way. While wearing boots wasn't a statistically significant risk factor for injury, it's interesting to note that 7 out of the 9 (78 percent) boot-wearers experienced injury or regular aches and pains and reported the most trouble at or below the knee. In contrast, only 39 of 62 (63 percent) hikers wearing low-top trail runners reported this type of injury.

ankle, which has negative repercussions on the knees, hips, and spine. Poorly fitting footwear also makes blisters more likely; this is covered later in the book. Both can bring an abrupt end to a long-distance hike. There's a lot to consider when buying footwear, so I've chosen to write exclusively about this process in chapter 3 on gear, rather than covering it here.

Warm up

Stretching is normally used to gain flexibility. Flexibility is the capacity to move a body part comfortably due to the ability of muscles and tendons to lengthen. In the sports world, stretching is a common practice for injury prevention because it is thought that someone who is more flexible is less likely to get injured. Recently, however, this notion has undergone fairly thorough scientific inquiry. As it turns out, there is little evidence to support stretching to prevent repetitive stress injury.

Why doesn't stretching help? Repetitive stress injuries often have little to do with flexibility, as they usually occur when a person is moving through normal body motions. Repetitive stress injuries have more to do with mode of use, frequency of use, and intensity of use. Stretching is likely to reduce the risk of repetitive stress injury only for people with abnormal or excessively limited flexibility, where normal body motions are significantly limited. This doesn't apply to most people.

Scientific evidence is emerging supporting the idea of warm-up exercises for injury prevention. Warm-up exercises, which involve active movement, can increase blood flow, lessen stiffness, and increase oxygen delivery to muscles while readying the nervous system for physical

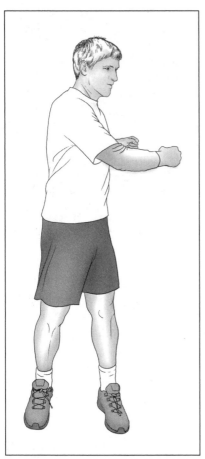

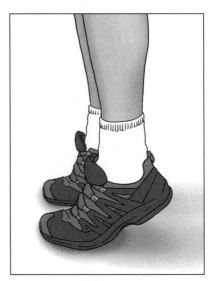

Above: *Trunk Twists: Rotate your torso 20 times to both sides while keeping your feet still.*

Above right: *Heel Raises: Rise up and down on your toes 20 times. Keep your knees straight.*

Right: *Lunges: Step forward and bend your knee 20 times. Keep your back straight. Repeat with your other side.*

activity. A quick morning warm-up routine will go a long way in preventing injury. My one-time hiking partner Germinator had a fairly elaborate warm-up routine each morning, and I never knew him to get injured. See the sample warm-up routine emphasizing muscles commonly involved in hiking.

Training

I get asked frequently by potential thru-hikers how to train for a hike. The simple answer is that most of the training takes place on the trail. There's really no way to replicate, through training, the physical and mental rigors of hiking from sunup to sundown for months on end—other than actually going out and doing it. That said, some physical preparation helps to better ease yourself and your body into the role of a hiker, and preparation is an important step in preventing repetitive stress injury. The following are some general tips. You should talk to your doctor or physical therapist about the right approach for you.

Improve your stamina for exercise. Having better stamina going into a hike will mean your body takes longer to fatigue. A fatigued body is a body more likely to be injured. While improving stamina by walking is ideal, most people don't have the kind of time to devote to walking long distances for training purposes. Jogging and cycling are good ways of improving stamina for hiking. Sports like soccer and tennis are also helpful, but tend to use muscles in a different way than with hiking. However, anything helps.

Strengthen your knees and ankles. Since the structures surrounding the knees and ankles are commonly injured in long-distance hiking, it makes sense to strengthen them prior to a hike. If you have a gym membership, incorporate heel-lifts and partial squats into your routine. Focus on low loads and high repetition. If you don't have a gym membership or prefer to train outside the gym, put on a pack and go find some stairs. A good starting point with stairs is to continuously walk up and down for 5 to 10 minutes without weight in your pack. You can build on this by progressively adding weight in your pack in 5-pound increments and increasing your time. If you can get up to 20 minutes with 15 pounds, you're doing well.

Lose weight. If you are overweight for your age and height, try losing some weight before the trail. Some hikers intentionally fatten up before hiking, but this isn't a good strategy if your aim is to reduce risk for repetitive stress injury. Added weight borne by the knees and feet increases injury risk.

Is losing five pounds of body weight the same as taking five pounds out of a backpack? No, it's better! Losing weight not only takes pressure off of the knees and feet, but it reduces the strain on the heart and vessels that have to supply blood to the body.

Whatever approach you choose, make sure you build up gradually as you don't want to injure yourself while training. Start with three times a week with days spaced evenly apart. Build up gradually to nearly every day over a period of two to three months, if you have the time. It's probably more important to increase things like time and frequency than weight or intensity.

Identify your intrinsic risk factors

When discussing factors that increase risk for injury, there are two categories to consider: extrinsic and intrinsic. Extrinsic risk factors are things external to a person that may increase the risk of injury. Walking over uneven terrain, wearing ill-fitting shoes, and hiking too many miles too quickly are examples of extrinsic risk factors because they are associated with the outside environment or a style of training. With the exception of training, this discussion on repetitive stress injury prevention has been centered on extrinsic risk factors like backpack fit and mileage. Intrinsic risk factors are characteristics within a person that increase the risk of injury. Intrinsic risk factors associated with repetitive stress injuries of the foot, ankle, and knee include obesity, excessive foot pronation, poor flexibility, previous injury, and poor physical fitness.

Obesity. An obese person is at a higher risk for a repetitive stress injury. The Centers for Disease Control in the United States defines adult obesity as having a body mass index (BMI) greater than 30.0.

> **BMI** can be calculated online using the U.S. Center for Disease Control's free calculator at www.cdc.gov under BMI.

Excessive foot pronation. Pronation is a complex movement of the foot during walking designed to absorb shock and prepare the foot to leave the ground. Everyone has a natural amount of pronation during walking, but some people pronate too much. Chronic, sustained overpronation can have negative consequences at the foot, ankle, knee, hip, and spine and has been identified as a risk factor for shin splints. The diagnosis of overpronation is typically made by a qualified medical professional such as a physician, a physical therapist, or a podiatrist.

> The best way to think about pronation is to imagine the ankle rolling inward and the foot flattening somewhat during the middle of a step.

Poor flexibility. Recall previously in this chapter that stretching was not a recommended warm-up exercise because most injuries take place within normal ranges of motion. However, if flexibility is so poor that normal range of motion is impaired, flexibility becomes a risk factor for injury and stretching might be an effective part of a warm-up.

Inflexibility that is significant enough to limit the normal motions of backpacking is rare in the general population. However, if you think you might be excessively inflexible, you may want to see a health professional such as a physical therapist, who can easily assess flexibility. When seeing such a professional, explain that you're planning a long-distance hike and that you're looking for excessively inflexible body parts. Everyone has some inflexibility, but in the context of preventing repetitive stress injury, it's the excessively inflexible body parts that prevent or restrict the normal motions of hiking that you should be concerned about.

Previous injury. Prior injury to a body part used in hiking, such as a fracture or a sprain to the foot, ankle, knee, hip, or spine may have created an abnormal alignment or force relationship between it and surrounding body parts. Long-distance hiking may aggravate this relationship, increasing the risk of repetitive stress injury.

Poor physical fitness. Poor physical fitness predisposes an aspiring long-distance hiker to injury. One reason is that the body will become more easily fatigued. Once fatigued, it is common for the body to begin to use parts or motions not ordinarily used in hiking to compensate for the fatigued parts.

A person who has one or some of the above intrinsic risk factors has a higher risk of experiencing a repetitive stress injury on the trail. It is important, then, to take preventive steps specific to intrinsic risk factors before starting a long-distance hike.

Obesity, poor physical fitness, and very poor flexibility can be simultaneously addressed by beginning a program of physical fitness two to three months before the start of a hike. Such a program can be prescribed by a doctor or a physical therapist.

People who excessively pronate often benefit from a shoe insert that supports the arch of the foot. Research has shown that it does not matter whether the insert is custom-made or off the shelf. It can be purchased at an outfitter or drug store.

People who have had significant prior injuries, especially to the foot, ankle, knee, hip, or spine should consult with their doctors before starting a long-distance hike. It is a good idea to see a doctor at least three months before the hike's start to learn how a past injury may affect your current way of walking. The discussion should consider what, if any, accommodations can be made to prevent injury.

On-Trail Management

Even after taking sound preventive measures, many long-distance hikers will still have to confront some type of repetitive stress injury while on the trail. Transforming your body from being fit to perform routines inherent in everyday life to being fit to perform the routines of a 20-plus-mile-per-day long-distance hiker can be a sudden and stressful remodeling, even for someone who is well prepared. Knowing the basics of how to manage a repetitive stress injury while on the trail can greatly increase the chances of long-distance hiking success, and surprisingly, most injuries are simple to manage without any sort of medical background. Being able to apply some of these basic concepts could stop an injury from lingering for your entire trip, as has been the case for some thru-hikers in the past. The graph describes how long it took for the injuries of 71 thru-hikers to heal. Eighteen percent of injuries never got better.

> Of the 13 people who reported that their injuries never got better, 6 reported a foot injury, 6 reported injuries to the knee or ankle, and 1 reported a back injury. One hiker lamented about a never-healed injury: "Constant foot soreness. On rest days and mornings I was reduced to moving with a severe 'hiker hobble.'"

The remainder of this chapter is dedicated to strategies for managing repetitive stress injuries while on the trail. These strategies are geared toward managing injuries of the knee, shin, ankle, and foot since these body parts constitute the vast majority of repetitive stress injuries to hikers. I won't give specifics about every possible kind of repetitive stress injury that can occur on the trail. For one, this would make a long and boring chapter. Second, and more importantly, while everyone experiences injury differently, the approach to on-trail repetitive stress injury management is similar regardless of the specific location of the injury. There are, however,

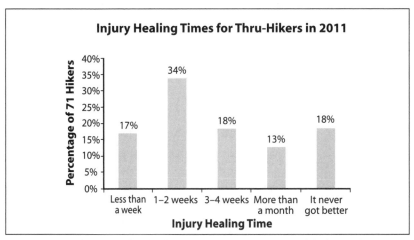

Seventy-one hikers who finished the AT or PCT in 2011 and had an injury reported how long it took to heal.

certain strategies that work best on a specific type of injury, and when this is the case I will make note.

Two quick disclaimers:

1. These strategies assume that injuries are in their early stages, where pain and discomfort might be better at some times and worse at others, but not at a constant or excruciatingly painful level. Injuries that are constantly painful, regardless of activity, or are painful enough to cause significant limping, should be taken care of off the trail with rest and possibly professional medical attention as they are past the point of on-trail remedy.
2. These are strategies for dealing with a specific class of injury: the repetitive stress injury, which frequently plagues distance hikers. These strategies are not for traumatic injuries. Injuries caused by trauma (i.e., a body part being damaged by something external to the body) are outside the scope of this book. To learn about how to manage trauma and emergency situations on the trail, I recommend picking up a good text on wilderness medicine and taking part in trainings and certification.

Management philosophy

At the core of managing any repetitive stress injury is the concept of unloading. Unloading means alleviating the burden on an injured body part by reducing the force it is required to produce or absorb, reducing the time spent in use, reducing repetitions, altering mode of use, or a combination of all four. Unloading allows a body part the best chance to repair and become stronger. The following management strategies provide methods for achieving unloading while on the trail.

Check your gear

The first and most obvious step in managing a repetitive stress injury on the trail is to do a quick assessment of the things that you're wearing. When it comes to repetitive stress injuries caused by gear, the two most likely culprits are footwear and backpacks.

Footwear. It's not unusual to experience a break-in time of at least several weeks for footwear, so keep this in mind if you think your shoes might be to blame. A common experience is to feel as though the shoe is too small or narrow for the foot or that the toes are cramming the front of the shoe. It is also common to feel as though the laces are too tight over the top of the foot. These sensations can come and go throughout the day and are usually the result of foot swelling, which is a normal adaptation to long-distance hiking. Foot swelling can also contribute to blisters where the swollen foot rubs against the shoe too much. Reducing a sock layer, wearing thinner socks, loosening laces, padding the feet in bothersome locations, and cutting strategic holes (as a last resort) are all ways that distance hikers manage the effects of foot swelling and discomfort.

One 2011 hiker writes: "[My shoes] wore out very quickly. [They] were done at about 450 miles, but I made them last until 550. The top of shoes at toes were completely blown out, and did not provide enough support, so the bottoms of my feet were very sore."

When looking at shoes as the potential source of a repetitive stress injury, you're really looking to see if the shoe has worn out or that it's truly a terrible fit. The worn-out shoe is easy to spot. The tread at the bottom of the shoe is gone and little intrinsic structural support inside the shoe remains. The tops of the shoes may have multiple holes. The shoe feels flimsy and likely has several holes that have gotten bigger over time. If you've got a worn-out shoe and your knees, feet, shins, or ankles are starting to bother you, buy new shoes.

Fit is a little more tricky to judge. This is partly due to the natural break-in period for feet and shoes alike, described above. On one hand, feet and shoes can adapt nicely during the break-in period and shoes will be comfortably worn for hundreds of miles thereafter. On the other hand, some shoes can truly be poorly sized, in which case the break-in period will do little but aggravate the bad fit. So there's a gray zone and each hiker has to find a limit to which he or she will tolerate problems from shoes.

Another way to get clues about bad fit is to look at the bottoms of shoes. Just as the wear pattern on a car's tires may signal problems with the alignment, if the bottom of a shoe has worn down in an unusual manner, this may suggest that the shoe has failed to do a good job supporting the biomechanics of your style of walking, contributing to a

> A PCT hiker writes: "I have wide feet, and my trail runners didn't fit well and ruined my feet in the first two days. I had to cut them open and had my boots overnighted to Julian."

pattern of altered use. Typically, shoes should wear a bit more on the outside of the heel compared to the inside. There may also be increased wear under or near the big toe. These patterns are normal and should not be a cause for alarm. What you're looking for are distinctly unusual patterns of wear, such as excessive wear on the inside of the heel, which may signal lack of a proper arch support. If you see such an unusual wear pattern and you're experiencing the beginnings of a repetitive stress injury, you may want to try making a temporary arch support (see page 125).

> B eing highly or moderately dissatisfied with the initial choice of footwear was reported by 19 percent of thru-hikers who completed the survey and finished the trail in 2011.

You will eventually need to get off the trail and get new shoes as there's no permanent on-trail solution to poor fit, and continuing to hike in shoes that are truly a poor fit could result in injury.

Shoes cost a lot of money, and it can be upsetting to discover that the shoes that fit perfectly in the store are not working out on the trail. However, pinching pennies and continuing to hike in poorly fitting footwear is a recipe for worsening injury.

Backpacks. Another potential gear-related source of repetitive injury can be from backpacks. At the start of a trail, you can expect sore shoulders and hips (sometimes even bruising) under pack straps. Major adjustments don't necessarily need to be made right away as sore shoulders and hips at the start of a trail are not usually due to poor fit. Rather, they are usually the result of the body adapting to its new backpack appendage and will often lessen over time. This is not to say that small, temporary adjustments cannot be made to relieve soreness. In the beginning stages of a long-distance hike I frequently loosen straps and unbuckle clips to give parts of my body a break and stay comfortable.

The biggest signs that a pack is truly a poor fit are aches and pains that do not lessen or that get progressively worse over several weeks. If left unchecked, these can become actual stress injuries either at the location of the pain or elsewhere in the body. Sometimes these constant aches and pains can be addressed with a simple pack adjustment such as tightening or loosening a strap. Since we can't always step back and see ourselves from a distance, having a companion look at how a pack fits is helpful in targeting a problem area and deciding which straps to tighten or loosen. Simply adjusting a strap may solve the problem. If you are unfamiliar with how each of the straps on your pack functions, it's a good idea to load up the pack before the start of a trail and practice tightening and loosening each strap. Learning how the straps change the way the pack feels will greatly increase your overall comfort on the trail.

Making a load adjustment or altering the distribution of weight inside a pack is another way of changing how a pack feels, although many long-distance hikers pack for convenience with only minor regard to how a load is distributed.

Finally, it's helpful to have someone take a look at your posture with your pack on. We commonly make adjustments in the way we stand when wearing a backpack. Since a backpack adds weight to the back, a common adjustment is to bend forward at the waist in order to keep the body's center of mass over the feet. Forward bending is more exaggerated with a heavier pack or a pack that sags below the hips. Other postural adjustments include thrusting the head and scrunching the shoulders forward. All of these postural adjustments can be reduced by lowering pack weight, making sure the pack rides up high on the hips, and tightening the hip belt around the hip bones. After you make these changes, have a partner look again at your posture to see if it looks different. Often, these changes will go a long way in relieving strain on body structures and the pain that often comes with it.

> Convenience packing means packing in such a way that more frequently accessed items are placed closer to the openings in the pack.

Sometimes, regardless of adjustments, a pack will continue to cause discomfort. This is an indication that perhaps it's time to get off trail and make a more thorough evaluation of what's going inside the pack, how much it weighs, and how well it fits. Doing so may mean the difference between a happy, comfortable hike and trail-ending injury.

Reduce pack weight

If you're being plagued by constantly sore hips, knees, ankles, or feet, reducing your pack weight can be part of an overall unloading strategy. Whenever I feel that I need to take a few pounds out of my pack, I first usually rank the things I'm carrying by frequency of use. Anything other than a single set of clothing used to protect me from the elements and equipment meant to provide critical first aid is a candidate for removal. Even inside my first-aid pack, I'll purge the extras and scrutinize. The same goes for warm clothes if I think I'm carrying extras. Do I really need two pairs of warm socks? Why do I have two hiking shirts if they just get dirty all the time?

Look for things that can do double duty. For instance, if you've decided to bring a potholder, can anything else in your gear double as a potholder? I've been using leaves, clothing, and sticks as potholders for years. If you're carrying a water bottle to hold water to be purified (by a SteriPen, perhaps), why not just use your cook pot? How about that knife? When was the last time you absolutely needed to cut something? And soap? Get rid of it. You shouldn't dump soapy water in the wilderness anyway. Anything that rides on your back should have to earn its keep. If you're looking for some suggestions from the thru-hiker crowd, review what a group of 83 thru-hikers carried for at least 75 percent of the entire trail, but in retrospect could have done without. Rain gear and extra clothing were the top choices, but 18

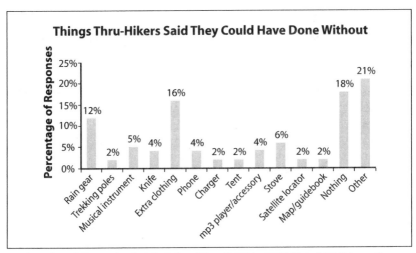

Eighty-three hikers who finished the AT or PCT in 2011 listed 85 things they could have done without.

percent of hikers said they needed everything they carried. Those who answered "other" provided the following responses:

- An extra pen.
- My iodine. I didn't really treat my water after I entered the Sierras.
- A bad-fitting backpack.
- Bandanna.
- Compass.
- Sketchbook and art supplies.
- Emergency matches and fire starter.
- Pants rather than shorts.
- A towel.
- Dental floss? I rarely used it. Bear rope, never used it once, carried it the entire way.
- Foot powder.
- Mousetraps.
- Neosporin.
- Cooking stuff.
- First-aid kit.
- Paper journal and pen; it was light but redundant since I could journal on my smartphone.
- Stuffed animal.
- Soap.

You can also trim a few ounces by cutting unnecessary straps and tags from gear. Just make sure you've got everything fit and adjusted to your liking first.

Finally, take an assessment of the food and water you're carrying. Is most of your food of an acceptable calorie density? (See chapter 1 on diet for details on how to choose proper foods to pack.) Are you getting to resupply points with lots of leftover food? If so, perhaps you're overpacking. Do you find yourself getting to water sources with lots of leftover water? If so, think of carrying less. Water weighs 8.3 pounds per gallon and is one of the heaviest things a hiker can carry.

Reduce daily mileage

Cutting down on the number of miles hiked each day is another part of an effective unloading strategy. Try cutting down by three to five miles for a week or two and see how your body feels. You can always make up for the lost miles over time. An easy way to reduce miles is to either cut your hiking day short or take longer breaks. But either approach works. Sleep in, take naps, have a long lunch in a pretty location—any of these approaches works. If you're out long-distance hiking, chances are that you're on vacation, so take it easy for a week or so and let your body heal.

Slowing down your speed of hiking is another way to cut down daily miles, but this is the least pre-

> **M**y own preference is to take longer breaks as I don't like getting to camp with lots of time left in the day. (I get restless.)

ferred method because it's likely that you're spending the same amount of time on your feet. It's better to take more breaks in the day. Of course, slowing down when accompanied by more breaks or a short hiking day is an excellent strategy.

Trekking sticks

Most long-distance hikers already carry trekking poles, but if you're one of those who don't, picking up a few poles or even some sturdy sticks can alleviate the load on painful body parts.

Downhill hiking

If it's your knees that are bothering you, try reducing your speed on the downhills. Don't pound or slap your feet, and take your time. If you have trekking poles, get them out in front of you to take some of the weight off your knees. Aggressive downhill walking can be a big con-

> **A** quote from a 39-year-old AT hiker at mile 68 in Georgia: "Knee pain . . . it is what it is! I don't mind lugging uphill, but knees aren't really designed to carry a load downward. I have tried to not rely too much on pain meds, just supporting it with a knee brace. Also, making sure I pace myself and take breaks–it's not a race each day!"

tributing factor to injured knees. This is especially pertinent on the Appalachian and other East Coast trails, which are comparatively steeper and have poorer footing than long-distance trails out west.

Take advantage of cold water

While not really an unloading technique, if you take your breaks near a cold stream, soak the injured body part for 15 minutes. Cold water on the surface of the skin will cause the underlying blood vessels to constrict, which has the effect of reducing any swelling that might be present. Cold water can also contribute to pain relief. Make sure you're also doing a good job of unloading the body part, as just using cold by itself won't help facilitate the healing process much.

Construct an arch support

An effective arch support can provide relief to painful knees and feet. If your hiking footwear has minimal support in the arch, you may want to try a supportive insole. It's often not feasible to leave the trail immediately and head into town to buy an insole. Thankfully, temporary arch supports can be easily fabricated on-trail from materials that are commonly carried by hikers. See page 125 for instructions.

Research on people with plantar fasciitis, a painful condition involving the connective tissue underneath the feet, has suggested that insoles supporting the arch of the foot alleviate pain and improve function.

During running, the Achilles handles peak forces of up to 12½ times body weight. This makes it a marvel of biomechanics, but also one of the more injury-prone body parts when it comes to backpacking.

Construct a heel lift

If your Achilles tendon is bothering you, a heel lift can provide effective pain relief. During walking, the Achilles tendon handles the highest amount of force of any body part, and it does so at a distinct mechanical disadvantage. The heel lift works by raising the heel slightly in the shoe, giving the Achilles tendon a greater mechanical advantage and thereby reducing the amount of force it is required to transmit. When using a heel lift, make one for both feet to maintain symmetry. Instructions for on-trail heel lift fabrication are on page 126.

Last thoughts on managing trail injury

These unloading techniques should give the body enough of a window to heal and strengthen, either instantly or in a week or so. If, despite all your best efforts to unload an injured body part, it gets worse or doesn't improve, then the best option is to take time off the trail. I've needed to take days off to give an injury a rest on both of my long-distance thru-hikes. On the AT in 2002, it was five days for knee pain. On the PCT in 2007, it was three and a half days for a fungal infection. There's never any reason to feel ashamed for taking time off to allow your body to heal. It's the smart thing to do and it's best to leave pride out of the decision making.

On a final note, you might wonder why I have not discussed the role of medications like ibuprofen (Motrin, Advil) and naproxen (Aleve) in managing repetitive stress injuries. Ibuprofen and naproxen are in a category of drug called non-steroidal anti-inflammatory drugs (NSAIDS). Many long-distance hikers rely on these medications for pain relief. I have

Construct an Arch Support
Arch Support Step-by-Step Construction

Materials Needed
- Foam
- Tape
- Writing tool
- Knife
- Plain shoe insole

Cut a rectangle of foam. If the foam can be flat, this is best. Otherwise, use what's available.

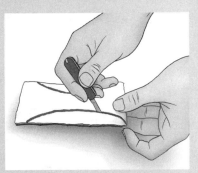

Draw two crescents, one slightly smaller than the other. The large crescent should be as long as the length of the arch of your foot. Cut out the crescents along the lines you drew.

Place the two crescents on top of each other over the space where the arch of the foot rests on the insole.

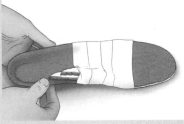

Use athletic or duct tape to secure the new arch support.

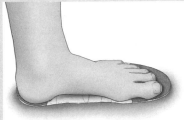

Be sure that the new support contours your arch. Make adjustments based on fit and comfort: Add or subtract foam or move foam forward or backward.

Construct a Heel Lift
Heel Support Step-by-Step Construction

Materials Needed
- Foam
- Tape
- Writing tool
- Knife
- Plain shoe insole

Finish trimming. Use athletic or duct tape to secure the heel lift.

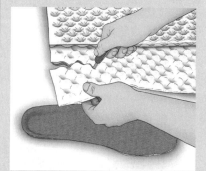

Cut a section of foam. Any type will do, but don't use overly thick foam to start with— ¼ quarter inch thick is about right.

Place foam over heel of insole, and begin trimming to shape.

The completed heel lift is ready for use.

chosen to not include these medicines in my recommendations for the management of repetitive stress injuries because current scientific research casts doubt on the presence of inflammation in many of these injuries.

Nonetheless, ibuprofen and naproxen are effective at relieving pain and widely used, regardless of whether or not inflammation is present. However, they do carry risks. For those prospective hikers considering using NSAIDS for pain relief, I advise consulting with a physician prior to beginning a long-distance hike. No medication should substitute for applying the core skills outlined in this chapter, for those skills are the true route to prevention and healing.

69 Thru-Hikers Describe Their Injuries

1. Overuse injury on my right knee from IT band stress.
2. Strained quads, pain aggravated by my fibromyalgia.
3. My IT band was tight, leading to a pinched sciatic nerve with back pain as a symptom. Probable cause was a backpack with structural inconsistencies, causing my muscles to overcompensate.
4. A journey of 5 million rolled ankles. Some of them fairly serious.
5. I had acute tendonitis in my ankle. I had to leave the trail to seek medical attention while in the Smokies. The doctor was concerned that if I continued hiking I would tear my Achilles tendon. I was not ready to give up so I did not take his advice. I decided to take 3 days off, and then I continued on crutches for 100 miles.
6. Tendonitis in ankle migrating to shin.
7. Knee pain on downhills.
8. Blisters, wrong shoe size (too small).
9. Persistent blisters on the Hat Creek Rim after we lost the snow.
10. Overuse injury of my hip joint due to the snow bank and acute injury to lower back due to slip and fall on hard ice.
11. My back ached on and off throughout my entire hike. I blame it to a misfitting pack.
12. Nagging soreness near ACL/MCL made it difficult to impossible to maintain typical hiking pace.
13. For a while I had infected blisters on the tops of my toes. Later on I had this weirdly large blister on my pinky toe that wouldn't go away for 2 weeks, limiting my hiking during that period.
14. Mildly twisted my ankle. Could still walk on it but had to wear a brace and put up with some pain.
15. Shin splints on my left leg.

16. Infected blisters on the heels and my Achilles tendonitis flared up in the first 250 miles.

17. I could not fully support my weight on my left leg, it would cause me to limp at camp until it got warmed up. If I pushed it too hard or did not favor it right/trip on it, I would experience terrible pain right below my knee cap and partially down the outside of my leg.

18. Blisters all over my feet in the hot desert. Gore-Tex shoes were a big mistake, not allowing my feet to breathe.

19. Pinched nerve from swollen neck discs, recurring problem/injury.

20. Blisters on my heels, toes, and feet. Nothing debilitating, but enough to make me doctor them every morning before walking with Vaseline and/or Band-Aids.

    Sun blisters on my hands (I hike with poles, so my hands were very exposed). I bought a thin pair of socks and cut out the toes, creating a sock glove so I could still use my fingers, but most of my hands were covered.

    Sunburn on my face, arms, and legs during most of the hike if I skimped at all or ran out of sunscreen.

21. Did not condition my feet before I made my decision to do the hike. Many blisters and aches early on and a constant struggle to monitor and compensate miles to keep feet at a functional level.

22. Pain in my left knee during the first two weeks of hiking, went away after I "got my legs."

23. Spilled pot of boiling water on back of leg. Had second-degree burn on back of my thigh, covering about half of it.

    Ingrown hair caused by rubbing of my pack and pants waistline on my hip.

24. I had knee surgery and now have knee pain.

25. Feet ached from not changing shoes enough . . . shoes worn out. And blisters from first pair.

26. My knee was in extreme pain, more so going downhill and bending it.

27. Ball of the foot was quite tender.

28. Foot tenderness, but nothing out of the ordinary, I think.

29. First metatarsal pain, present before the trail but very painful until my feet broke in the first few weeks.

30. I didn't really suffer too much while hiking the PCT. The worst was probably a few blisters, sunburns, and pack rash on my back.

31. Knees ached after prolonged hiking, even with a light pack. During zero days in town I'd feel it the most; stretching out my legs hurt my knees! Didn't really feel any pain while hiking; only when I stopped for breaks and had to get up or when I finished hiking for the day. It took a good month after my thru-hike for the aches to disappear. I've since learned I could do some knee exercises that may be effective in preventing the knee aches.
32. Sore feet! Didn't have to stop because of it, but definitely felt it by the end of each day.
33. Too much weight and too long a time in too tough terrain with too little ankle support made both my ankles hurt. Sharp pain coming in stings.
34. Plantar fasciitis. Morton's syndrome. Inflamed nerve in the toes.
35. Feet swollen and sore after several days of hiking in wet socks.
36. Many badly sprained ankles.
37. I had really bad blisters from the Smokies to Damascus. Made walking very painful.
38. I developed plantar fasciitis.
39. Sprained ankle, severe shin splints, knee problems for last quarter. Sprained ankle I never let completely heal, knee lasted 2 weeks. Shin splints lasted 3 weeks.
40. Stress fracture (most likely) in both feet at different times. The 500 miles of snow in the Sierra helped ice the first, which started due to depending on my left foot more as I had a shin splint on my right leg.
41. Poison oak and ingrown toenail surgically removed.
42. Sprained ankle.
43. Groin pain (internal swelling of veins) took about a week to heal. A constant ache in the joint of my big toe lasted the remainder of the second half of the hike.
44. Aches in ankles throughout trip at the end of long days.
45. Shin splints.
46. Ankle sprain.
47. Tingling feet during day, aching feet at night.
48. Sore tendons in feet and loss of feeling in toes.
49. I-T band soreness.
50. Shin splint.
51. Shin splints. From Pearisburg to Waynesboro. Most painful on dragon's tooth.

52. Left shoulder hurt most of the trail from previous injury.
53. Tendinitis of the Achilles and EDL tendon.
54. I suffered shin splints for two weeks with one week one shin the other week the other shin, consecutively.
55. An ankle surgery that I aggravated in the Sierra and it hurt and rolled on me the rest of the hike. Just starting to heal three months later . . .
56. I hit my knee floating the South Fork of the Kern, and got a dent in my cartilage. This caused sharp pain when I used it the wrong way, or sometimes it hurt with every step. I treated it with glucosamine.
57. Thought I had a bad knee even before the hike. The hike made me break through it and it never hurt after the third week.
58. Rolled right ankle multiple times in Washington. Long-term damaged toe extensors on left foot from having shoes too tight to compensate for weak right ankle from rolling.
59. General knee ligament pain from repetitive motion. Shin splints and plantar fasciitis were close seconds.
60. Severe shin splint; I took five days off in Yosemite Valley plus another seven days off when I got to Lake Tahoe before I could hike pain free.
61. Constant foot soreness. On rest days and mornings, I was reduced to moving with a severe hiker hobble.
62. I began to get terrible pains in my arch and on my left foot the bones really hurt. I may have had a stress fracture but never got it checked out. It only hurt after mile 15 of the day. It hurt until I got home and stopped doing high-impact workouts.
63. Bad ache along the interior of my left scapula due to a broken pack.
64. Shin splints, torn muscle, something like that. Had no insurance so just hiked through the pain. Oh, also broke my pinky but that never bothered me.
65. Sharp sudden pain in center of knee, followed by painful walking for several days. Four or five episodes of such after four high-mile days in a row.
66. Rash, lower back. Started infected for almost four months and leaked pus and was irritated by wearing a backpack.
67. Feet hurt toward the end of the trail.
68. Lower back muscle knotted like a mofo.
69. Torn ligament.

6

Skin Care

Of all the problems I've had to manage while hiking long-distance trails, skin injuries have been the most painful and debilitating. Had it not been for the walk-in clinic in Santa Clarita, California, and the generosity of the Saufley family in Agua Dulce, an unbearable skin problem would have derailed my 2007 PCT thru-hike. Within my first week on the PCT, I developed red marks on the inside of my upper thighs that quickly grew in size and became excruciatingly painful each time I began sweating. Attributing it to simple chafing and anxious to head the problem off before it got worse, I got off the trail where it crossed California Route 78 and hitched a ride into Julian, where I purchased Gold Bond powder, zinc oxide cream, and Huggies wipes at the suggestion of a fellow hiker.

Back on the trail, I took care to stay clean using the disposable Huggies wipes in their handy plastic container. I liberally applied Gold Bond and found relief . . . until sweat washed it away, leaving me in pain once again. The zinc oxide proved to be of minimal use as sweat washed it away also, providing only a temporary reprieve from what was becoming a progressively worsening condition. All attempts at cleanliness didn't seem to matter.

I tried to avoid sweating as much as possible, going slow on the climbs and making miles in the cooler parts of the day, but sweating was unavoidable in the southern California heat and the problem continued to worsen. Another hiker gave me some Bag Balm and again, I got some relief from the pain, but when I started sweating in earnest the Bag Balm melted away and the pain returned. The stinging became unbearable.

I walked into Big Bear City a desperate man. I had heard from other hikers of a product called Bodyglide that was made for runners to eliminate chafing. I hopped the city bus over to the outfitter on the other side of town only to find out that they had closed early for the Mother's Day holiday and were not open the next day either as it was Sunday. I did not have plans to remain in Big Bear City until Monday. There happened to be a Kmart nearby, so I took the bus over and spent the next hour scanning the shelves of the first-aid aisle looking at various ointments, lotions, and lubricants that might be able to provide permanent relief. I settled on two unlikely products: Desitin (for diaper rash) and Astroglide (for "personal" lubrication). I paused thoughtfully at a bottle of Vagisil, remembering some advice from a female hiker. Yes, I was desperate, but not quite ready to take *that* step.

Back on the trail, I began trying my new products. The Astroglide was an instant failure. It was a slippery mess to put on and soon melted away to leave an unpleasant tackiness that only made the pain worse. Next up was Desitin, the diaper rash destructor. This proved to be the most effective solution to date as it lasted a good while and made the pain go away. I applied liberally. Since Desitin has zinc oxide as its main ingredient there seemed to be very little difference between the Desitin and the zinc oxide I had bought back in Julian. I was puzzled as to why the Desitin lasted longer; maybe it was the fish oil in the Desitin. Whatever the reason, Desitin helped take the edge off, although the redness didn't go away.

By the time I arrived at the Saufley's Hiker Heaven hostel in Agua Dulce, 454 miles up the PCT, the pain was manageable, but the problem had grown so large that a substantial red, cracked section of skin covered both my inner thighs. Clearly the problem was not going away, and it was time to seek professional help. The Saufleys kindly lent me one of their vehicles, and I drove to the walk-in clinic in Santa Clarita. The on-duty physician took one look at my skin and knew precisely what the problem was: a fungal infection called tinea cruris, aka jock itch.

I had been mistaken all along. This was not a simple issue of chafing. Somewhere along the way, I had picked up a fungus that flourished in the moist environment of my inner thigh. Left untreated, it had festered away over the course of the month, growing steadily. No wonder the remedies I had tried were ineffective. None was an antifungal agent, and as helpful as Desitin was, it only dulled the pain temporarily. The physician prescribed ketoconazole, which is a powerful prescription antifungal cream, and asked that I apply it twice a day. He noted that it might take two to three weeks to work. I went straight to the pharmacy, picking up the biggest bottle of it that was available.

Over the next several days, the fungus showed no signs of disappearing and the stinging pain persisted. I took time off at Hikertown, a squat, dusty hiker hostel on the western edge of the Mojave Desert with a tiny patch of lawn, an outdoor shower, a bit of shade, and a few cabins. Watching all my thru-hiker companions pass me by was hard to bear, but I needed the time off to heal, so I passed the days by sorting piles of nails, learning about fungal infections online in one of the hostel's demobilized mobile homes, showing other hikers around, and borrowing the caretaker's car to make marathon runs to the Sizzler on I-5. After 3½ days at Hikertown I was kicked out because the caretaker had to leave on a job assignment and closed the hostel. Not completely healed and with nowhere to go but through arguably the hottest desert section of the PCT, I had arrived at what proved to be the low point of my thru-hike. It could only get better from here.

I woke up the following morning outside the chain-link fence that surrounds Hikertown and began walking with a red Mojave sunrise on my right. As the physician told me, the redness began to recede over the following week. The pain went from constant to occasional, and I didn't feel it in so many places. I stopped using Desitin, and by the time I got to Tehachapi Pass, 112 miles from Agua Dulce, the infection had nearly resolved. I continued using the antifungal medication even after the infection disappeared completely, applying it daily all the way to Oregon as a preventive measure. The problem did not reoccur, and looking back, I wished I had been smarter about managing the problem. When my own remedies didn't work, I should have sought professional help sooner, rather than continuing to suffer.

This chapter describes how to manage some common on-trail problems that affect the skin. Like bones, muscles, and ligaments, the skin also takes a beating on a long-distance hike. Most of us who live and work in industrialized societies aren't used to being outside in the elements all day and might not be prepared for what comes our way on the trail. The skin, just like the rest of the body, needs some time to adapt to its new routine. Additionally, being out on a trail for many days on end puts hikers at risk for certain skin problems.

This chapter covers three categories of skin problems: fungal infections and chafing, blisters, and poison ivy/poison oak. Sunburn, another skin-related problem, is covered in chapter 8.

Fungal Infections and Chafing

Although not exactly the same type of problem, fungal infections and chafing fall under a single category in this book because management is similar. Long-distance hikers are prone to a few types of fungal infections. Jock itch, or *tinea cruris*, describes a fungal infection in the groin, inner thigh, or anal area. Athlete's foot, or *tinea pedis*, is a fungal infection of the feet. In both instances, the skin becomes cracked, itchy, flaky, and often painful, particularly when sweating occurs. Fungal infections can occur in other parts of the body, particularly anywhere that stays warm and moist, such as the armpits.

> Abrasive skin rubbing or chafing will break down the surface of the skin and make it more vulnerable to an opportunistic fungal infection.

For distance hikers, the feet and the inner thighs are the most at-risk areas for fungal infection because they are enclosed spaces that are constantly in motion, creating both heat and moisture, which are favorable conditions for fungi. Depending on your body type, these areas can also be prone to chafing. Logically, then, the best way to prevent a fungal infection is to effectively manage chronic heat and moisture generation as well as to manage chafing or rubbing of the skin. You have to expect a certain amount of chafing on a long-distance trail. Skin, just like bones and muscles, must get used to its new routine and toughen up. If it's a particularly rainy trail, problems with chafing can be magnified as water helps macerate and break down layers of skin that rub together. But a small amount of chafing doesn't become an avenue for an opportunistic fungus. You just have to keep the chafing under control.

Lubricants and anti-rubbing products are helpful in reducing the damaging effects of constant moisture and salts from water and sweat on the skin. There are a large number of products on the market—which to use depends on your own preferences and experiences. Whichever product you choose, apply it at the beginning of the day, before sweating begins. Apply the product anywhere rubbing and excessive sweating is expected. Common areas are the feet, groin, inner thighs, and inside the buttocks. Reapply during your lunch break, especially on days when you expect to sweat a lot or

> I prefer Bodyglide, which comes in a small stick shaped like deodorant and is easy to apply and clean.

during an all-day rain. In cooler climates or during the winter, you'll generally sweat less, and one application of anti-rubbing product will probably be enough.

When chafing either grows worse or doesn't go away, look for signs of growing redness, cracking, or scaling—those are signs of a fungal infection, and it may be time to begin applying a topical antifungal medication.

Lots of these are available over the counter, and a pharmacist should be able to point the way. If the problem continues to worsen despite these preventive measures, it's probably time to see a physician, as I did, for prescription-strength medication.

> I tend to sweat a lot and am susceptible to fungal infections, so I make a habit of applying a small amount of antifungal cream at the end of a day of hiking and apply Bodyglide more than once during the day.

In addition to lubricants and antifungals, other preventive measures that cut down on chafing and the occurrence of a fungus include the type of clothing you wear, good hygiene, and being aware of how fungus spreads.

Clothing

Tight, compressive pants or underwear made of a fabric such as cotton that tends to hold moisture will create a moist, warm environment that fungal infections thrive on. I have settled on a pair of Nike Dri-Fit running shorts with a liner for hiking. They wick moisture away from my body, are light as a feather, and have a thin layer of fabric in the liner to cut down on rubbing. Don't ever hike in cotton on a long-distance trip. It retains moisture and, when wet, both lowers body temperature and adds considerable weight. It also takes a long time to dry. Avoid cotton and look instead for materials that move moisture well. Many synthetic fabrics fit this description and they're available in most outdoor retailers.

Hygiene

It goes without saying that keeping your hands and body clean will reduce the risk of infection. I usually carry a 1-ounce trial size bottle of hand sanitizer with me.

Fungal infections are contagious. If you share clothing or food with other hikers, make sure everyone's hands are sanitized. I know hikers who refuse to accept food from other hikers or shake hands. While this might be taking prevention a step too far, long-distance hikers are a notoriously filthy group and a little extra caution doesn't hurt when it comes to staying healthy on the trail.

Blisters

Blisters are another one of those nearly unavoidable consequences of long-distance hiking. It is rare to encounter a distance hiker who has not had to manage some type of blister. For hikers, blisters usually occur somewhere on the feet as these are the parts of the body where the skin is most exposed to repetitive trauma.

On the trail, blisters are usually caused by either excessive friction, impact, or pinching. (Blisters can also be caused by poison ivy, oak, or sumac. More on this later in the chapter.) Friction blisters are caused by repeated friction on the skin generated by excessive rubbing against surrounding material or other body parts. The most infamous of all friction blisters is the posterior heel blister, located at the back of the heel where the Achilles tendon attaches. Other popular locations for friction blisters are at the tops of the toes and feet, between the toes, and the balls of the feet.

In 2011, blisters were listed as the most difficult aspect of the trail by 14 of 43 (33 percent) PCT hikers at mile 454.

Impact blisters are caused by the trauma of repeated impact with the ground. Common locations for impact blisters are on the outside of the heels and the bottom or sides of the great toes. Pinch blisters can happen when the skin is pinched together on a repetitive basis. Toes are a common place for pinch blisters.

In all instances, the body is responding to cell damage to the outer layers of the skin. As skin experiences repetitive trauma, cells die and/or blood vessels rupture and a fluid-filled sac (blister) results. The sac can contain either blood or pus. The blood or pus is contained in a thick layer of cells designed to protect the underlying damaged area of skin. With continued trauma to the skin, pus accumulates and the blister grows larger. Blisters are highly sensitive to touch and pressure. Hiking with even a small blister can be a painful experience.

Pus is a creamy protein-rich fluid containing dead cells that are not readily reabsorbed into the body's circulatory system.

Blisters should be addressed immediately. Failure to properly treat a blister will not only result in a painful hike, but may ultimately lead to infection if the trauma causing the blister shears the skin enough to create openings in the skin. If untreated, the blister is likely to grow wider, or blisters can form on other parts of the foot as the hiker compensates to try and avoid pressure on the current blister. For friction blisters, the telltale warning sign is a hot spot.

Hot spots are red marks on the skin that do not readily fade away and are typically painful. The redness associated with a hot spot is a sign that the skin is getting inflamed. During a hike, if one area of your foot or ankle starts to feel painful or irritable, chances are high that a hot spot is developing. A hot spot will most certainly lead to a friction blister if you don't reduce the friction that is causing the hot spot to develop.

If you suspect you have a hot spot, the best thing to do is to stop hiking and inspect the skin. If a hot spot is present, either remove the irritant (sometimes simply a fold in a sock or trail debris is causing the irritation) or add a protective barrier between the skin and the cause of the hot spot. A protective barrier can range from adding or taking off a sock to using one of many off-the-shelf blister products (mole skin, mole foam, and so on) or the hiker's favorite—duct tape. If you are using an adhesive product, make sure your skin is clean and thoroughly dry first or the product will quickly fall off or fail to adhere altogether. Adhesive qualities often improve if you rub the tape lightly after putting it on. Do not put adhesive tape directly over an open wound, skin tear, or abrasion. Doing so invites infection or worsening of the opening when it comes time to remove the tape.

> I prefer using plain athletic tape, as it seems to be more resistant to peeling off during wet conditions than duct tape.

Problems with friction are sometimes solved by adding a sock liner, which is a thin sock that goes on underneath the hiking sock and purportedly cuts down on rubbing. Keep in mind that heat and moisture exacerbate skin damage caused by friction. Wearing breathable shoes and socks that fit well goes a long way in preventing hot spots and blisters. Impact and pinch blisters are generally not preceded by hot spots.

If a blister does appear, the best thing to do is to drain the fluid by popping the blister. If the blister remains filled with fluid, you'll have less room in your shoe for your foot, causing the problem to get worse or a new problem to form. The stagnant fluid inside the blister may also become infected. Draining a blister is not rocket science or advanced field medicine. The procedure is simple, and you can do it by yourself.

> I've had success with sock liners and add or remove them frequently with the changing needs of my feet. I've sometimes even placed them outside my hiking sock.

1. Prepare the blister by cleaning it thoroughly. Small alcohol wipes or alcohol-based gel is good for this.
2. Heat the end of a small, sharp object, such as a safety pin, over a flame for 10 seconds.
3. Insert the object into the base of the blister where it meets the intact skin. Fluid should begin to flow out of the hole you made.

4. Drain as much fluid as possible. Pinch and squeeze to get every last drop.
5. Once again, clean the skin and allow it to dry.
6. Place a small pad of sterile gauze over the drained blister and cover it with either athletic or duct tape. Don't put the tape directly over a drained blister.

> I don't have much faith in waterproof tape. It's expensive and its adhesive properties don't stand up when it comes to the repetitive stresses and strains of distance hiking.

Again, be certain to try and remove the cause of the blister or mitigate the friction causing it if possible. In cases where no obvious irritant stands out, the skin may need to simply toughen up. This is usually the case with impact blisters. The blister may have to be drained multiple times before the skin adapts to its new role and grows into a callus.

Poison Ivy, Oak, and Sumac

Poison ivy, poison oak, and poison sumac have long been a source of agony for the wayward hiker. These plants produce oil called urushiol oil that causes an itchy, oozy allergic rash that doesn't ever seem to go away. The best way to avoid the poison ivy, oak, and sumac rash is to remember what the plants look like and avoid them

> According to the Poison Ivy, Oak, and Sumac Information Center (http://poisonivy.aesir .com), it takes just a billionth of a gram of urushiol oil to induce an allergic reaction.

at all costs. Fortunately, they aren't difficult to recognize. If you're not keen on plant identification, the mantra "leaves of three, let it be" is sound advice for avoiding contact with poison ivy and oak. However, poison sumac, which mostly grows east of the Mississippi River, has leaf clusters of seven to thirteen, so some skill with identification is still important.

If you do happen to develop an allergic rash, the easiest way to manage it is to stop in the next town and pick up some lotion. Special skin lotion is made for these types of rashes, and it's easy to find in even the most basic pharmacy. Follow the directions on the tube, and you should be OK. It's important, if you do contract an allergic rash, to keep the area free from dirt and grime and clean it regularly. Just like any other cut or blister, the rash is an opening in the skin that can serve as an entry point for bacteria. Finally, if you feel as though you may have touched poison ivy, oak, or sumac, take care not to touch your face until it is washed off. Take it from me, a giant swollen face is no fun!

7

Frame of Mind

So far I've outlined important skills for maximizing the chances of having a successful long-distance hike. What I haven't addressed is what many thru-hikers consider to be the single most important part of finishing a long-distance trail: having the right frame of mind.

Lots of prospective thru-hikers set out on the long trails each year with visions of peaceful gurgling brooks, brilliant sunsets, and lofty mountain ridges. Every day is 75 degrees and sunny, perhaps with a few puffy white clouds, and nighttime is filled with the sounds of crickets chirping as the hiker sleeps a sound, comfy, dream-filled sleep in the great outdoors. The volumes of books romanticizing the long trails, either through professional photographs or well-crafted prose, reinforce these visually and emotionally fulfilling moments.

Is it wrong to have these dreams and expectations? No. Long-distance hikers will experience all of these things along with many more natural wonders and adventures. Is it dangerous to think that every day on the trail will be like this? Yes. A long-distance hike occurs over many weeks or thousands of miles. Books can fail to mention the hard parts of hiking, and stories of cold and misery are often given a quirky punch line or woven into tales of bravery, deceiving the reader about what days of cold and rain really do to the body and psyche.

In our daily lives, we all use mechanisms to get us through tough times. These mechanisms help us overcome marital issues, stay satisfied at our jobs, or finish a race. As a long-distance hiker, you need adaptive mechanisms so that bad times on the trail don't result in a snap decision to quit. Bad weather combined with the novel stress and strain of chugging over the mountains in north Georgia during the spring is notorious for causing aborted AT thru-hikes. The unprepared novice long-distance hiker gets a taste of body ache, bad weather, and bone-chilling cold, decides "this isn't for me," and goes home. The novice's error is failing to consider the big picture, which is that eventually the temperatures will go up, gear will dry, and hundreds of miles of spectacular scenery and sunny warm days are ahead. The successful long-distance hiker keeps everything in perspective and realizes that long-distance hiking is a marathon (many, actually) and not a sprint. It is a mindset of inevitable perseverance, coupled with intelligent decision making along the way.

So far, I've outlined strategies for smart decision making on the trail. To ultimately be effective, though, these strategies need to go hand in hand with keeping a sharp mindset under psychologically negative circumstances. Common negative circumstances are addressed in this chapter, with some suggestions about how to manage them.

Physical Discomfort

There is no such thing as a completed thru-hike without physical discomfort at some point. Expect to encounter pain, cold, heat, hunger, exhaustion, and thirst—among a host of other ailments. Sometimes these discomforts are temporary, disappearing with changing weather, a rest break, or a cool drink of water. Occasionally, though, they'll last longer, signaling actual injury or a condition that must be properly managed for the long term.

The first weapon in mitigating physical discomfort is to take proper preventive measures. A substantial portion of this book has been about skills to manage and prevent physical discomfort. Applying sun block and wearing long clothing will prevent painful sunburn. Reducing pack weight and having well-fitting footwear will reduce musculoskeletal strains and stresses. Packing the proper foods will mitigate hunger and keep energy levels high. However, even when you take all of the proper preventive measures, you can still expect physical discomfort. There's just no easy way to go from a normal civilized lifestyle to the daily physical grind of a long-distance hike. Knowing this, then, is a reminder that you not only need to have the skills to manage and prevent physical discomfort, but also the mental preparation.

Being mentally prepared for physical discomfort doesn't mean being able to blindly ignore pain, cold, and fatigue while relentlessly plodding on down the trail. Quite the opposite. Being mentally prepared means being ready to manage whatever physical discomfort comes your way. The key part of this is being ready—that is, having realistic expectations about the physical strain a long-distance hike can have on the body. If you are expecting to experience cold, pain, and fatigue at some point along your journey, then when they happen you'll be able to move right on to managing the problem, hopefully using some of the skills learned in this book. If you believe you can complete a hike without experiencing any of these discomforts, you will be unprepared to manage them when they occur. You'll be taken by surprise. Common misperceptions include believing gear will always keep out the rain and the cold or that pre-trail conditioning will make you immune to injury. These are naive expectations. Mental preparedness for pain and discomfort is a crucial strategy for success. Expect to be uncomfortable from time to time, and pat yourself on the back when it's minimal.

Boredom and Loneliness

You can also expect periods of bore-dom or loneliness on a long-dis-

> There are many more interesting parts of Pennsylvania, but not where the AT goes!

tance hike. Anyone away from home for such a long period of time will miss loved ones. In the more remote parts of some trails or when hiking late in the season, it can be rare to even see a single person for consecutive days. As odd as it may seem, the reality on long-distance trails is that not all parts of the trail are scenic, and some parts can be downright ugly.

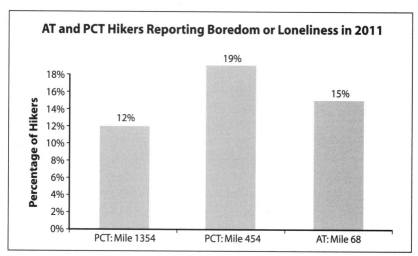

In 2011, 231 AT and PCT hikers were asked what the top three most difficult aspect of the trail were at three different mile points.

In order for the national scenic trails system in the United States to boast continuous, unbroken hiking trails for thousands of miles, trails must sometimes pass through uninteresting scenery. Sometimes this is man-made: a trail may need to run along a road, shoot through a culvert under an interstate, or bypass more scenic land that happens to be on private property. Other times, a trail is just in a section of the country that isn't all that interesting. AT hikers lambast poor Pennsylvania, whose section of the trail is rocky and predictable with few scenic views. PCT hikers complain about the endless winding canyons in southern California and the sometimes uninteresting landscapes of southern Oregon, where Mt. Shasta never seems to go away. If you are setting out on a long-distance hike, expect periods of boredom and loneliness and have some strategies in place so that you can enjoy your hike, even when the landscape is less than appealing. The following are some common strategies I've employed or seen others using.

Carry portable music

When I hiked across Pennsylvania in 2002, I carried a small AM/FM radio. Pennsylvania's unimaginative rock-strewn ridgelines were boring for hiking, but they were great for radio reception. Getting through blazing hot northern California was much easier when I allowed myself one hour with my digital music player each day.

Portable music is the subject of some controversy amongst hikers. Long-distance hikers who carry portable music are sometimes criticized for being unappreciative of the trail's natural beauty. I can understand this perspective and, to a small degree, agree with it. It's definitely an issue I struggle with: Am I so dependent on modern technology that I need to listen to my iPod to enjoy the wilderness? Why can't I just enjoy the smells and sounds around me,

> Thru-hikers seem to be split on the value of portable music, based on the 2011 survey: 49 percent reported carrying portable music for more than 75 percent of the trail, and 51 percent did not.

even if the views aren't good? I rationalize my decision by keeping the big picture in mind: I want to finish the trail and enjoy myself while doing it. Portable music is one way of breaking up the monotony of a day without much scenery or getting me into a good mood when I'm feeling down. I usually limit my portable music time to one hour per day, two hours tops.

Another way to rationalize carrying a portable music player is to understand that historically speaking, long distance travelers have always brought along portable entertainment, whether it be a deck of cards or musical instruments. Sure, a beat-up guitar looks like it fits in a little better on the trail than a chrome-plated iPod, but they both serve the same purpose.

A final tidbit about portable music: Be extremely cautious about wearing headphones when passing through areas where rattlesnakes are known to live. The rattlesnake's rattle is its best defense, and if you can't hear it because of Bob Marley, you're inviting trouble.

Make friends

My normal hiking style is to hike solo. If I encounter another hiker who is going my pace, I might hike with him or her for a few days, but ultimately I move along or fall behind. I credit my friends Optimist, Stopwatch, Germinator, and NoCar for helping me get across northern California in 2007, which was a very hot, dry, and tiresome section of trail for me. I broke from my usual style and made an effort to stay with them all the way to central Oregon. I had to increase my hiking pace to cover about 30 miles per day (up from 27), but by then my body could handle the pace, and the pleasure of their company was well worth the extra effort.

Make side trips

Long-distance hiking trails are chock full of interesting side trips to towns or other areas of interest. On the PCT in 2007, I scaled Mount Thielsen and Mount McLoughlin to break up the generally flat, hot, landscape. The adrenaline rush I got clawing up the precipitous rock atop Thielsen and summiting McLoughlin at sunrise were both big highlights for me and made south and central Oregon much more exciting. Plenty of folks take a zero day (a day without hiking) when they get tired of the trail. These are both healthy ways of fighting boredom and keeping a positive frame of mind about the trip.

Read and write

Both reading and writing are good ways to beat loneliness and boredom. Pick up a newspaper in town

> Of the 85 successful thru-hikers who completed the 2011 survey, 66 percent brought a journal and 40 percent brought reading material more than 75 percent of the way.

and carry it along. Buy a book, cut it up into sections, and send it along in a mail drop. Even if you don't use mail drops, the entertainment value of a good book is often worth its weight and bulk in your pack. I kept a journal for the PCT and wrote plenty of letters and ideas, including the speech I gave at my brother's wedding.

Bring along a special treat or luxury item

Having that special item in your pack that makes you happy will go a long way in dealing with boredom and loneliness on a long-distance trail. The graph shows what hikers in 2011 brought along to keep themselves happy. The responses in the "other" category are listed below:

- My town dress!
- Spot [satellite messenger]
- My stuffed squirrel "Snow Cup"
- Light-up Ultimate Frisbee—Mexico to Canada, baby!
- Deodorant
- Soda, music, and herb
- My video camera
- Flip flops. Could have done without them to save a few ounces but was really glad I had them. Especially while showering in town.
- Nail scissors and small mirror. Not essential but was so happy to have them.
- Glissading sled
- Roll your own cigarettes
- I was minimal so I don't think I had a luxury item.
- A proper double-walled tent instead of a tarp

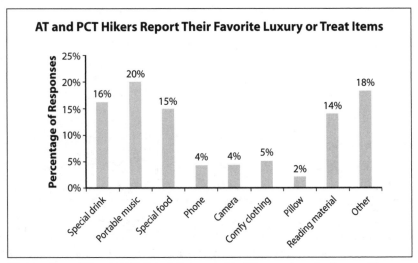

Eighty-three AT and PCT thru-hikers provided 93 responses to the question, "What was your favorite treat or luxury item to have along on the trail?"

- My own bed in a motel room
- Ukulele
- Journal
- Laptop

Impatience and Frustration

There are lots of long-distance journeys out in the world for those who crave adventure. Thousands of people each year participate in long-distance cycling, running, or adventure racing. Hundreds of thousands of people fly to foreign countries on vacation. These are all faster ways of travel than long-distance hiking.

Walking is the slowest way of getting from one point to another on two feet. The average walking pace of a long-distance hiker is somewhere between 2.5 to 3 miles per hour. That's slow! What prospective long-distance hikers sometimes fail to realize is that walking long distances takes time. Pity the poor hiker who struggles through the first 100 miles of a trail and arrives into town in high spirits, which are quashed when the hiker looks at a map and realizes how little distance he has actually covered in comparison to the entire length of the trail. AT, PCT, and CDT hikers can expect to take 4 to 6 months to finish. This is a wide range, and plenty of people finish at either end of this range as different hiking styles and paces take shape.

It's a big mistake to start a long-distance trail already thinking about the end. Progress will seem impossibly slow, and finishing the trail will appear hopeless. If I had started the AT thinking about Georgia every day, I probably would have quit. Nonetheless, it helps the spirit to know that progress is being made on a hike, so a good way to do this is to make smaller goals. I typically have a number of goals in mind when I'm hiking. When I started the AT, the longest goal I had was covering the 300-plus miles to New Hampshire. I also looked forward to getting to the next town in Maine (Monson), getting to camp at night, getting to lunch, and getting to a spot where I could have a snack and some water. I always

Trail	No. of Thru-Hikers Responding to Survey	Average No. of Days	Range
AT	26	161	59–225
PCT	57	154	96–187

Time Spent on Complete Thru-Hikes in 2011

thought of something to look forward to, as it helped me feel like I had accomplished something and made progress. I didn't start thinking about the finish in Georgia for quite a while. Some people have even smaller goals when they hike, like a spot where the trail turns a corner, a mountain pass, the next blaze, or even the next step. Whatever you choose for trail goals, realize that it's important to have them and that being able to break them down into smaller, more manageable goals is a key to finishing any long-distance hike.

8

The Elements

One of the most frightening and dangerous nights I've had in the wilderness was a night where I was caught unprepared to deal with the elements in Washington's Goat Rocks. I had spent the entire day walking through a dreary cold drizzle, and my trail guide indicated that there was a shelter (one of just a few on the entire PCT) close to my mileage goal for the day. As evening approached and I began climbing up toward the shelter, I became enveloped in a thick fog, and the drizzle was unrelenting. As darkness began to fall, the temperature dropped into the upper 30s. I noticed small stands of evergreens through the thick fog as I made my way above tree line and toward the shelter. Using my altimeter and my watch as guides, I arrived at 7:00 p.m. where I believed the shelter should be. Unfortunately, no shelter was to be found. Although I had set my altimeter earlier in the day, I decided that because of the low-pressure weather system my altimeter was reading a higher elevation than actual and I chose to hike on with hopes of encountering the shelter soon.

I continued on through the evening over trail cut through rock and snow with fog lingering thick and darkness quickly falling. The trail started to climb steeply over rocks, but I reasoned that I was on the right path as my map showed the shelter to be near the height of trail elevation in this area. As 8:00 drew near, I began to worry that I had passed the shelter and become lost. Drawing near to the crest of the climb, I fixed my limited sight upon a sign in the distance, hoping to be set back on track. Upon reaching the top I peered at the sign and saw only weathered wood. Whatever had been written on the sign had slowly disappeared over the years by exposure to wind and rain. It was now very dark, and I was officially lost with the temperature hovering in the high 30s with a steady drizzle.

I was well above tree line with a shelter and sleeping system that was dependent on trees. (At the time I slept under a tarp, which I strung up to trees, and a bivy sack.) Even with my headlamp, visibility was poor and I was exhausted, so I decided to make camp. I did my best to string the tarp under large boulders before crawling into my down bag and bivy for the night.

As the night passed, wind and rain came through with enough intensity to whip my tarp violently, loosening and sometimes disengaging my rope from the rock it was tied to. Rain got under my tarp, soaked the outside of my bivy, and began seeping into my sleeping bag, rendering the down insulation useless. Periodically, I had to get out of my sleeping bag to reattach a rope or urinate, and each of these experiences was a test of willpower as each meant exposing my damp body to 30-degree temperatures and drizzle or rain. I was freezing cold, shivering, alone, and miserable.

Toward the early morning hours, I lay face down with my arms under my chest to stay warm, waiting for the first hint of daylight so that I could see and make my way out of the Goat Rocks. Day finally broke with the fog still thick. I quickly packed up, jumping up and down to try and generate warmth. Everything was wet, including my down jacket. Luck, however, was on my side. As I rounded the rock pile I had camped beside, the

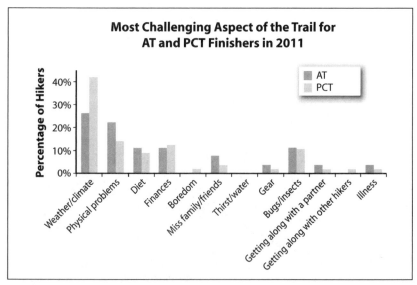

Twenty-seven AT thru-hikers and 57 PCT thru-hikers completed the survey. The year 2011 was an especially high snow year on the PCT, which may have skewed the results somewhat.

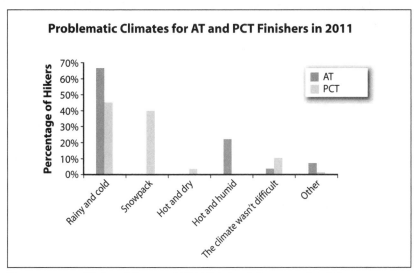

Problematic Climates for AT and PCT Finishers in 2011

Twenty-seven AT thru-hikers and 58 PCT thru hikers completed the survey. The year 2011 was an especially high snow year on the PCT, which may have skewed the results somewhat.

fog lifted, revealing a magnificent green valley and the iconic snowy glaciers that dot the Goat Rocks. The breach in the fog bank also revealed a thin ribbon of trail wrapping itself around the side of a scree slope far below. I had wandered off trail, about 500 feet above where I should have been. The shelter, I later found out, didn't exist. It had been removed years before. I safely made it out of Goat Rocks to the gas station at White Pass that day and considered myself lucky to have not succumbed to hypothermia that night.

From the freezing cold rain and snow of a Georgia spring to the blazing heat and shadeless desert of southern California, the elements could be the greatest challenge long-distance hikers face. Weather and climate were the most difficult aspects of the trail for AT and PCT thru-hikers in the 2011 survey. Weather and climate also topped the list of most influential reasons for not finishing the AT or PCT at 22 percent. Most respondents indicated this was due to the high snowpack in the Sierra Nevada.

Because you have to hike most long-distance trails over several seasons if a thru-hike is your goal, encountering less-than-ideal weather through a variety of climates and environments is inevitable. Taking the time to be familiar with and adequately prepare for variations in climate markedly increase the chances of success. This chapter provides some important tips on protection from the elements and staying comfortable. While weather can come in all varieties, 2011 survey respondents identified three patterns as most problematic: rainy and cold, hot and humid (on the AT), and snowpack (on the PCT).

Rainy and Cold

Hiking in 35-degree dry weather is chilly for sure, but a brisk pace and warm clothing will soon make the walking enjoyable. A rainy 35 degrees is an entirely different scenario. Water can rapidly conduct heat from the skin, making the 35-degree air temperature feel like an arctic winter. This presents a very real danger for long-distance hikers. Hiking in this type of weather isn't just about staying warm, it's also about staying dry. It's important to be vigilant about keeping yourself and your gear dry in order to prevent hypothermia.

Layering

Layering refers to wearing multiple layers of clothing for weather protection instead of a single piece of clothing. Each layer serves a specific purpose and can be used either by itself or in combination with other layers, depending on conditions. Layering is more versatile and efficient than using a single garment, which can be bulky and whose various components cannot typically be used separately. For cold, wet weather, there are three important layers: outer, middle, and inner.

Call me old-fashioned, but I don't trust materials that claim to be completely waterproof and breathable. The best way to avoid moisture buildup inside a garment is to open zippers or slow down. Most modern-day outer shells are equipped with underarm zippers for venting. Don't rely on high-tech materials to do this job for you.

The outer layer is what keeps precipitation and wind from penetrating to the body and the inner two layers. It should be composed of some type of waterproof and windproof material. Water- and wind-resistant outer layers may be acceptable, but might not hold up in a deluge.

The middle layer is responsible for minimizing heat loss from the body and should be composed of warm, insulating material such as down or thick fleece. Consider a vest design if you tend to sweat easily.

The inner layer, worn closest to the skin, helps keep the body dry by moving moisture away from the body. It should be composed of some type of moisture-wicking material. That's it! Isn't it funny that entire industries are dedicated to high-tech clothing when in reality, a smart, three-layer clothing strategy is all that's needed?

Take care of the hands and head

A weatherproof hat is crucial for preventing heat loss through the head. Gloves are helpful for preventing the misery of freezing cold fingers. For the hands, layering a warm mitten with a weatherproof overmitt is helpful to prevent the warm mittens from getting soaked and useless. For the legs, generally some warm, skintight leggings are sufficient. The legs are not nearly as important to keep dry and warm as the head and chest during a cold rain because the legs are in constant motion and generating a substantial amount of heat on their own. They are also well insulated by muscle, fat, and contain groups of fairly large blood vessels.

> For me, rain pants don't offer much added value for their weight and volume. Many brands get heavy when they're wet and legs can generally stay comfortable in leggings, which are lighter when wet and more pleasant to walk in.

The feet? Eh.

Probably the worst thing about a cold, rainy day is having feet that feel like blocks of ice. This is when the day hiker with heavy waterproof boots may look quizzically at the distance hiker in trail runners. I believe the daily lightweight comfort of a trail runner is well worth enduring chilly feet on a cold, wet day. I also believe that trying to keep feet dry during a day (or a week) of hiking in rain is a waste of time. The happy medium is to get trail runners that have some Gore-Tex in them. Just know that these shoes will be slightly heavier, more expensive, and hotter than trail runners that do not contain Gore-Tex, and even these will ultimately give way to water during a day of hiking in rain.

Keep dry and wet gear separate

Maintaining a set of designated dry clothes is critically important. Since carrying the added weight of many sets of clothes is usually not in the cards for hiking long distances, a good strategy is to carry two sets of clothes: one for hiking and one for camp. The camp clothes should generally be warm and should be kept dry. During bad weather, it's important that this separation is meticulously maintained. Not having dry clothes to change into at the end of a cold rainy day is an open door for hypothermia. While it's disheartening to start the day in cold, wet hiking clothes after a night in dry clothes, it's the smart move. A brisk first mile will often warm the body up and take the initial chills away.

Be sure to keep wet and dry items separated inside the pack. Items such as sleeping bags that are made of down quickly absorb moisture if they are not kept separate. A

W hile hiking, I like to stash my wet gear outside my main pack compartment for extra separation from my dry gear.

wet down bag is useless. A soaking wet tent fly will soon soak everything around it. Garbage bags or jumbo-sized zipper-lock bags (found at some moving van rental stores) help keep wet separate from dry.

Keep moving

The body heat generated from hiking is important for staying warm in cold, wet weather. Those midday hour-long naps have to be set aside as laying around in a cold rain means setting up shelter, getting out of hiking clothes, and putting on dry clothes. After the nap, getting back into cold, damp, hiking clothes that have cooled to air temperature is no fun at all. Brrrrr! A better strategy is to take shorter, more frequent breaks

I like to carry a small silnylon tarp that is easily deployable and can be strung up to create a quick waterproof shelter to take short breaks under on rainy days. In lieu of a tarp, the boughs of evergreen trees provide good protection from rain.

or end the day early and listen to the rain patter on your shelter from the coziness of a dry sleeping bag.

Drink water

It seems counterintuitive to drink water when water is falling all around, but just as one can drown in an inch of water, dehydration can strike in a rainstorm. Eating is also important for maintaining energy levels and body heat during the day. Rather than taking long lunches and risk getting cold, many short snack breaks composed of easy-to-digest foods like salty crackers and pretzels are the key to getting through a dreary day.

Don't sweat

When hiking vigorously or over steep terrain wearing rain and thermal wear, the body will heat up and want to start sweating. It is important to prevent this from occurring during rainy, cold days. Sweating is the body's way of cooling off through water evaporation, and on a cold day, sweating accelerates the process of hypothermia. The best way to avoid sweating is to use the aforementioned layering system, where you add and remove layers to keep your body from sweating. Hiking in cold, rainy weather is a continual process of adjusting to heat, cool, and reheat the body. It can

> Hats work too! I like to raise my hat to the very top of my head or even remove it to expose my forehead to help me cool down without sweating.

get tiresome to constantly be stopping to unzip and rezip, but the consequence of being soaked in sweat on a rainy, cold day is hypothermia.

Hot

While cold and wet weather is a more familiar set of dangers for hikers, the hot weather experienced during peak summer months is an equally potent danger worthy of careful consideration. The consequences of dehydration, heatstroke, and severe sunburn are serious and can lead to the end of a long-distance hike. The strategies for protecting yourself in hot weather follow the same themes as cold, wet weather, but with different, sometimes opposite recommendations.

Dress right

The right clothing for hot weather depends on the level of tree cover. On the PCT in 2007, I started the trail wearing a sleeveless black shirt made of high-tech breathable fabric. Despite religious use of sunscreen, the nasty sunburn I developed on my shoulders after a week on the trail convinced me I had made the wrong choice. Realizing I could not continue going sleeveless, I was forced to switch to the other shirt I was carrying; a midweight, long-sleeve, moisture-wicking shirt with a half zipper in front. The original intent of packing this shirt was to stay warm on chilly desert nights. Instead, it became my primary daytime desert shirt, despite its weight and color. I wore it every day all the way to the Canadian border. The shirt moved moisture exceptionally well and the long sleeves and thicker material kept the sun off my body.

Protective clothing is a must in conditions where, due to lack of tree cover, prolonged exposure to direct sun is expected. Sun will dehydrate the body by evaporating moisture from the skin and compliment sweating to accelerate the dehydration process. Sunglasses and a broad-brimmed hat are also a priority. Long pants, again, are optional and don't add much more protection from the sun as legs are often in the shade of the body and backpack and do not tend to bear the brunt of the sun's direct rays unless the sun is being reflected off snow and ice.

The opposite approach is best if you are under constant forest canopy, where continuous direct sun exposure is not a threat. Most of the AT fits this description, so dressing for hot weather on the AT means minimizing clothing to aid body cooling and reduce moisture loss through sweating.

> When I hiked the PCT through southern California, I often took long naps in the middle of the day (under shade) to avoid walking in the extreme heat. I usually made the best mileage in the early morning and evening hours.

Slow down and hydrate

Particularly in the middle of the day, which is often the hottest part of the day, take care to rest often and drink plenty of water.

Flex your hours

Adding to the last point, being flexible with a hiking schedule can be an effective strategy for dealing with the heat. Night hiking is a strategy sometimes employed by distance hikers to beat the heat. I am not a big proponent of night hiking since this strategy has its own set of pitfalls (the need to use a headlamp, lack of scenery, lack of companionship unless you have a partner, and it's easier to get lost). I'm much more enthusiastic about quasi night hiking. That is, waking up at 4:00 or 5:00 a.m., hiking for a few hours before eating breakfast, taking a long midday nap at lunch, and hiking several hours after dinner until dark. Both night hiking and quasi night hiking are effective ways of staying cool in the heat and, by default, are also ways of preventing dehydration as water demands are less in cool weather.

> Another form of quasi night hiking is to sleep and then hike for four hours at a time. This is *not* an effective strategy and results in overtiredness. Sleep should be had all at once to be most effective. Adding up a few hours here and there to make eight hours isn't the same as getting eight hours of continuous sleep.

Snowpack

Along the long-distance trails of the continental United States, heavy snowpack doesn't typically get to the point where it becomes a major climatic hindrance for hikers. The year 2011, however, turned out to be a high snow year in the western United States. In fact, it was such a big year that a small handful of folks left the PCT due to the staggering amounts of snow. In other years, the snowpack tends to be more benign. The year I hiked the

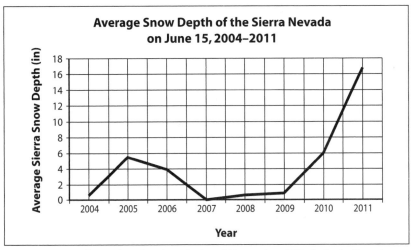

Source: *National Weather Service, National Operational Hydrologic Remote Sensing Center*

PCT, 2007, was one of the lowest snowpacks on record, and I recall easily making 25-mile days through the High Sierra, which is unheard of in a high snow year. The graph shows the average snow depth in the Sierra Nevada on June 15 over the eight years spanning 2004–2011. Clearly, there's some variability from year to year.

Those who stuck it out on the PCT in 2011 had a lot to say about the snow in the High Sierra:

- Frosty the Snow-Devil doesn't know the difference between July and January!
- The snow was challenging—ice chutes were really scary and being 4'11" the rivers nearly killed me so I skipped north from Bishop to Truckee.
- Snow is a hard thing for a body to walk on all day long—especially 10 hours straight. I was mentally ready for it all, but all of that sliding and putting your breaks on and falling was harsh.
- Good year for water and cool in the desert, but very high snow year in the Sierras. This made for physically hard hiking (through snow) and required more time for route finding. The toughest section was Tuolumne to Sonora Pass, with very high and challenging river crossings. This year's hikers are 2+ weeks behind those in a more "typical" year.

There's no easy way of dealing with big snowpack. A few words of wisdom:

Walking: Take it easy

The most obvious problem faced by hikers in big snow years is actually walking over snow. Snowpack at high elevations can go on for miles and miles. Snow can make climbing passes agonizing, and walking through fields of sun cups is tedious and tough on the body. Postholing, a term for what happens when your legs sink down through snow, is incredibly frustrating. Other than carrying crampons and an ice axe, which are essential for safety, the best advice to follow is to slow down, relax, take breaks, and don't expect to cover big miles.

> In 2011, a very high snow year for the Sierra Nevada, 106 PCT hikers filled out a survey for this book at mile 1,348 in northern California. Fifty-one hikers (48 percent) reported problems associated with Sierra Nevada snow as being the most challenging part of the trail so far.

Navigation

Lots of 2011 PCT hikers described difficulties with route finding in the High Sierra. In a high snow year, the actual trail can often be deep under snow, and you'll have no indication of which way the trail goes other than a map or guidebook. It's always important to learn basic map and compass skills for wilderness travel, even in the age of GPS. It's even more important to be able to use a map and compass in high snow years, when knowing how to read topography and how to identify key map points can be a huge time saver. Of course, following the snowy footprints of others is always a handy guide too, but you may also wind up following the mistakes of others if you're not careful.

River crossings

One of the most enjoyable things about long-distance hiking is that you're out in the wild for most of the time; away from roads, cars, and crowds. Consequently you're also away from many of the rules designed to maintain order and create an environment of safety that are found in popular parks. Out on the long trails, no one tells you where you can't go or puts ropes out for your protection. You're

> The best time to cross a snowmelt stream is at the beginning of the day, when streams are often at their lowest levels.

free to slide down a snowy slope, hop under that waterfall, or go wandering off over a ridge top just to see what's on the other side. But this also means that your safety depends on the quality of your judgment. River crossings during high snow years can be especially hazardous due to the massive quantities of snowmelt. If you don't feel safe crossing a high river, you can do one of two things: walk upstream to try and find a safer location to cross or wait for another person to come along. If you're on one of the sparser trails, you'll probably need to try the former. Whatever you do, don't attempt a crossing solo if you don't feel safe.

Skip ahead

Skipping ahead means moving ahead on a trail when you come across poor conditions and then coming back to finish the skipped section when conditions have improved.

For those of us who are purists, this idea is blasphemy. For those of us who are capable of exercising common sense, it's a legitimate

> A purist hiker insists on hiking every step of the official trail route in a continuous fashion.

choice in high snow years, when deep snowpack and dangerous fords make hiking through high elevations treacherous and time consuming.

9
Animals

Major wildlife encounters (bear, deer, elk, mountain goats) on long-distance hikes over established trails in the United States are infrequent. This could be because many hikers are moving quickly, looking down at the trail, and making noise. It is also likely that many animals have become accustomed to seeing humans on these trails and tend to stay away. Nonetheless, wildlife encounters are frequent enough that knowing how to properly act is important to ensuring a safe and enjoyable long-distance hike and reducing the likelihood of something running off with all the food! Most animals encountered on long-distance trails in the continental United States are harmless and slither, scamper, or fly away at the first sign of human approach. Others are not as shy and will leap at the opportunity to steal as much food as possible during the night or even in broad daylight. If any animal perceives a sufficient enough threat, it is capable of attacking a human. This chapter addresses managing common animal encounters while hiking on trails in the continental United States. It also addresses one of the most obnoxious and hated animal presences on trails: bugs.

Bears

I look forward to the opportunity to spot a bear. Bears might be the most exciting animal to see when hiking, owing to their large size, curious habits, and perhaps that tiny rush of fear from being around a wild animal that is much faster and stronger than us (but thankfully not as smart). If I were to guess how many bears I've seen on over 5,000 miles of trail, I'd put the number somewhere between 20 and 30. In some cases, I saw the bear from afar, perhaps a few hundred feet below me along a streambed.

In other cases, I have come across a bear right on the trail, and if it didn't see me, I got to watch as it went about its business. In most cases, however, the bear spotted me and quickly bolted. I've never had a negative experience with a bear, although this hasn't been everyone's experience.

In subarctic North America, long-distance hikers can expect to encounter two species of bear: the American black bear and the brown bear. The American black bear (*Ursus americanus*) is by far the more populous of the two bears, with numbers in the many hundreds of thousands. Black bears can be found near long-distance hiking trails from coast to coast and have been spotted from northern Mexico to just north of tree line in Canada. Grizzly bears, which are a subspecies of the brown bear, are fewer in number and have a much smaller range, existing mostly in Canada and Alaska. In the continental United States, grizzlies range in the northern Rockies, Yellowstone National Park and vicinity, and the northern Cascades in Washington. Consequent to the sheer difference in numbers, most bear encounters on long-distance trails in the United States are with black bears.

> In the 99 years spanning 1900 and 2009, only 63 people in North America have been killed as result of an encounter with a black bear. Of these encounters, only 14 occurred in the continental United States. Scientists believe that this may be due to the fact that black bears are more widely hunted in the lower 48 than in Canada and Alaska, thus causing them to have a greater fear of humans.

While they can be a thrill to encounter, bears also present two problems to long-distance hikers: theft of food and risk of attack.

Black bear attacks are extremely rare and the risk of a fatal attack in North America is less than minuscule.

The incidence of grizzly attacks is also extremely low. In Glacier National Park, Montana, only 9 people have been killed by grizzlies since 1967. Fewer than 10 people have been killed by grizzlies in and around Yellowstone National Park since the early 1900s. The National Park Service estimates the chances of being injured by a bear while in Yellowstone National Park as 1 in 1.9 million. When comparing the number of injury-causing incidents with their much smaller relative population in relation to black bears, grizzly bears are widely thought to be the more aggressive bear species around humans.

It has long been thought that bears become aggressive around humans to defend their young, although this is only partly true. With grizzlies, this has, in fact, been the case as the majority of fatalities associated with attacks have involved a female defending her cubs and often involved a surprised bear. In contrast, recent scientific evidence shows that most fatalities from black bear attacks have come not from a female defending her cubs, but from predatory attacks by males, who are known to range farther and take more risks than females with cubs.

> A 2003 study about grizzly attacks in Alberta, Canada, found that grizzlies involved in injury-causing events with humans were first seen at a distance of less than 50 meters.

With both types of bear, the fact remains that injury-causing attacks are extremely rare in North America. Bears fear and avoid people, and the great majority will disappear at the smell, sight, or sound of an approaching hiker.

The best way to avoid a dangerous encounter with a bear is to take steps to let bears know your presence. When walking around blind corners in areas populated by bears, yell or shout to warn bears of your approach. It's also important to sleep away from where you cooked your meal and to store your food far away from your campsite as human food and trash have long been considered bear attractants.

Sighting a solo bear often means the bear has failed to notice you. In this case, do not startle the bear. Stop hiking and enjoy watching the bear go about its business, but be sure to keep a good distance away and don't startle the bear. Most often, the bear will ultimately smell or see you, become frightened, and run away. If the bear has noticed you and does not run away, clap your hands or shout to let it know that you're not to be trifled with. If you encounter a bear and her cubs, try not to position yourself between them and back

> Bear spray is sold in pressurized cans and typically contains the chemical capsaicin, a derivative of the chili pepper.

away slowly so as not to startle the bear. Do not run away or remove your pack. Bears run fast, and packs provide body protection. In the rare instance a bear charges, stand your ground and return the aggressive behavior. Yell, clap, and shout at the top of your lungs. Throw sticks or rocks. This can be enough to convince a charging bear that you're not worth the risk. Also, a charging bear will often bluff, veering away or brushing by you at the last minute.

Another way of preventing injury from a bear is to carry bear spray. Using bear spray is generally supported by science—as of 2012, no bear spray has ever been present at the scene of a fatal black bear attack. However, this is far from definitive scientific evidence. As a long-distance hiker, the decision to carry bear spray involves assessing your tolerance for risk.

Knowing that the risk of a fatal attack or serious injury caused by a bear is low and understanding how to take preventive measures to deter such attacks, you have to weigh the peace of mind that comes with carrying bear spray with the weight and pack space taken up by the spray. There's no right or wrong answer. It's a personal risk-tolerance decision.

> On my last trip along the CDT in Montana, I picked up bear spray after hearing reports of recent fatal grizzly attacks near Yellowstone. By the numbers, it was an irrational decision, but I don't regret carrying bear spray, especially during nights I slept alone. I felt safer with it, and therefore the weight (11½ ounces) and space taken up by the spray was justified.

The more likely problem posed to hikers by bears is theft of food and the destruction of gear associated with the theft. Bears have a strong interest in food brought into the wilderness by hikers and are persistent at obtaining it. The simple explanation for this behavior is that during the summer and fall, bears are driven to consume large quantities of high-calorie food in preparation for hibernation. They normally pack in calories through a diet consisting of berries, nuts, and grubs, but they certainly wouldn't turn down a candy bar or two.

There are a number of methods to keep bears from hiker food, and the most effective method largely depends on location. For portions of long-distance trails that are well outside of popular state and national parks, where bears can be hunted by humans and have a lower exposure to humans, bears have not learned intricate methods for getting to human food. In this case, hanging food in a stuff sack from a tall tree limb is sufficient.

> A study conducted in the Lake Tahoe area of Nevada was able to show that deterrents such as rubber bullets, pepper spray, and dogs were ineffective in keeping bears from coming back to areas where human habitats (and their trash) were present.

The counterbalance method has been widely acknowledged to be the most reliable way of hanging food. However, the counterbalance method requires a good deal of skill and time, not to mention sticks of the right length and the ability to balance two food sacks of about equal weight. (Step by step instructions can be found online.) I find this method to be more trouble than it's worth, especially on those long days when I roll into camp just before dark with just enough time to eat dinner, pitch camp, and hit the sack. Who wants to go fumbling around with the counterbalance method? Not me. So when camping in an area where bears are not known to bother hikers, I have found that a simple rope thrown up over a tall tree branch (about 20 feet up) with a food bag tied to one end of it will often suffice, and I've never had a problem with bears or any other animal when using this method.

I don't advocate using this hanging method when a trail passes through a popular park where bears are known to be less shy around humans. Some of these bears have learned that humans mean food and have figured out how to get food bags down from tree branches, even when the counterbalance method is used. Most popular national and state parks with significant bear populations have systems in place for keeping bears away from hiker food, and it's important to follow these systems. Expect to encounter and use devices such as metal lockers, pulleys, or poles with hooks to secure food away from bears. However, if a trail passes through a popular park that also doubles as a federally designated wilderness area, you may not find such devices as they are not in keeping with the concept of wilderness. To solve the bear problem, some parks are now mandating the use of bear canisters.

Lots of long-distance hikers collectively groan when it comes to bear canisters. And why shouldn't they? Bear canisters add weight, and they're bulky to carry, which doesn't fit with a streamlined, ultralight method of travel. The biggest canisters often accommodate no more than about six days' worth of food, placing a limit on a hiker's range. Naturally, then, distance hikers have devised methods for circumventing canisters, the most popular of which is sleeping with food under their heads. I have known PCT hikers who, so appalled by the idea of hauling a bear canister, have done this in problem bear areas like Yosemite. Most of the national park rangers I have spoken with have thoroughly rejected this as a safe practice. While it's true that the PCT passes through the more remote areas of some national parks like Yosemite and the likelihood of a bear going for food under a hiker's head is probably low, all it takes is one hungry bear to cause a catastrophe, and for this reason I'm an advocate of bear canisters. In fact, in recent years I've started using bear canisters outside of traditional problem bear areas because I believe the advantage of carrying a bear canister outweighs its weight and size disadvantages. Consider:

Canisters make protecting food easy and worry free. Once the canister is sealed and placed on the ground away from the campsite, all is taken care of. No more worrying about bears climbing trees or chewing through rope. No more time wasted trying to hang a bear rope or lifting a bag onto a hook in the dark.

Many canisters are waterproof. No more wet food bags!

Mouse proof. Canisters are not only bear proof, but they protect against mice, porcupine, deer, and any other animals as well. They're even ant proof.

Use as furniture. Some canisters make a nice table, seat, or camera tripod. When not full, many canisters can double as a waterproofing container for clothing or sleeping bags. However, you don't want your sleeping clothing or bag smelling like old food, so use caution with how you store non-food items in bear canisters.

Organizational aid. Canisters are a convenient way of keeping food contained in a backpack and insulate food well. (I've never had a melted candy bar in my bear canister.)

No trees needed. At high elevations where bears are still present, trees can be short and have downwardly sloped branches, providing few options for hanging food.

The downside to a bear canister is, of course, the weight and volume it takes up in a pack. However, my BearVault BV 500 fits nicely into a mid-volume pack, and large canisters similar to this model should fit inside most backpacks intended for multiday trail travel. Weight is really the biggest consideration. Models that have been approved by land managing agencies weigh no less than 2 pounds and make a significant contribution to pack weight.

A way to circumvent the weight of a bear canister is to carry a bear bag, a tough sack made of a rugged fabric resistant to a bear's teeth and claws. These models weigh less than a pound. But as of this writing no fabric-based bear bag is currently approved by the National Park Service in areas where carrying a bear canister is mandatory. Hikers on the PCT should know that the park service mandates carrying bear canisters along several sections of the PCT in the Sierra Nevada range, including all of Yosemite National Park and a large swath of the Ansel Adams Wilderness.

I suspect that bear canisters will only continue to gain favor among state and federal agencies that manage public land. Canisters put more of an onus on the hiker to be responsible, rather than relying on the usually cash-strapped agencies to maintain systems of pulleys and heavy metal food lockers. Canisters are also more in keeping with leave-no-trace wilderness ethics.

Keeping food away from bears also means exercising a little common sense. Since bears are attracted by smells, hikers should avoid sleeping in the same place where they cook. The sleeping area should be scoured of all traces of food or items that could be seen by a bear as food. This means packing and stowing away not only food, but empty wrappers and trash, toothpaste, and toothbrushes.

Bears can be one of the highlights of a long-distance hiking trip if you understand their behavior and exercise common-sense techniques for protecting your food and yourself.

Bugs

I spent my childhood in Bowdoin, Maine, a rural town of small farmsteads and stubborn soil. I remember spending spring and early summer afternoons outside on our lawn playing Wiffle ball with my brother and some of the kids who lived on the road. While I was not the best hitter and never got to pitch, my enjoyment of the game was buoyed by the inevitable brawls that would erupt between my best friend and his brother over strikes and balls, safe and out. They were nasty brawls, almost always ending in crying, shouting, and sometimes blood. The brothers would scrap and punch and go tumbling onto the ground, every once in a while involving one of us in the fray. It would all come to an end, however, once the early evening rolled around and the mosquitoes took flight. Lost Wiffle balls would go unfound and games stopped before the home team had its "last ups" on account of the mosquitoes being so bad that they swarmed around our faces and got in our eyes and mouths. Standing still to wait for a pitch meant being a sitting duck for the clouds of skeeters that would descend upon you.

Armed with this experience, I chose late June as the start time of my southbound AT thru-hike. To have chosen May or early June would be to have doomed myself to unending swarms of black flies and mosquitoes. That year, which was thankfully one of the driest on record, I didn't run into too many bad bug problems. The bugs in Maine were past their peak, and by the time I got to Vermont I could comfortably sleep in shelters without having to worry about being harassed at night. Others haven't had it so lucky.

While timing is a good strategy for dealing with bugs, a long-distance hiker will inevitably need other tools to combat bugs since a three-season thru-hike of a major trail takes many months for most people and wetter-than-normal seasons amplify the bug problem. This means that for some of the time on the trail, bugs will be bad.

A good first weapon in keeping bugs from biting is to cover up. Wear long sleeves, a hat, sunglasses, and pants. Some hikers use bug nets over their faces as well, but I've never found this to be very enjoyable.

The next weapon in the hiker's arsenal should be a good insect repellant. When it comes to keeping the bugs off, there are two highly effective compounds, DEET and permethrin.

N,N-Diethyl-meta-toluamide, thankfully abbreviated DEET, is the most common ingredient in insect repellants worldwide. It is usually found in various concentrations, the most potent being somewhere around 95 percent. High DEET-based repellants come in small 1- to 2-ounce sizes and can be applied in small doses to the neck, arms, shoulders, and legs. Periodic application of a DEET-based repellant will do a good job keeping insects, especially mosquitoes and ticks, at bay for a period of time (how long depends on DEET concentration). A warning for using DEET or any other chemical that is absorbed into skin: Don't apply it while sweating. I met a man on the AT who, in desperation, had applied a large quantity of Ben's 100 to his shoulders while completely drenched in sweat. He was not a happy man as the stinging was unbearable.

A more lightweight and effective choice for repelling insects is permethrin. Unlike DEET, which repels insects, permethrin is an insecticide that kills insects on contact. Another way that permethrin is different from traditional repellants is that permethrin is applied to fabric like tents and clothing instead of the skin. It

Permethrin is derived from the chrysanthemum flower. It is thought to work by blocking insect nerve transmission.

can be applied to tents, shirts, jackets, hats, or any other piece of clothing by either washing or spraying on a permethrin solution. The compound is harmless to humans, harmless to fabric (will not affect water resiliency), and one treatment will last up to six months.

Campfire smoke also acts as a natural insect repellant, so those traveling with wood-burning stoves have an additional advantage. Sorry alcohol and canister stove-users, bugs don't seem to mind biting you over your boiling mac and cheese.

Finally, avoid harassment by being on the move when bugs are at their worst. Summertime affords long days for hiking, and bugs are usually most active during the dusk hours. A good strategy is to eat dinner in the late afternoon and then hike through dusk, making camp just before dark after the bugs have died down. Also, avoid camping in areas like swamps, marshes, and lakes, where there's lots of standing water.

Bees, Hornets, and Wasps

When considering the most dangerous animals to humans in the United States, bees, hornets, and wasps probably don't spring to mind. However, the scientific data suggests that bees, hornets, and wasps kill more people each year than any single animal in the United States. From 1991 to 2001, bees, hornets, and wasps accounted for 533 deaths, 27 percent of all animal-related fatalities (excluding instances where people rode animals). This was more than double the incidence when compared to dogs, which accounted for 11 percent of fatalities. This might come as a surprise to hikers, who are accustomed to bears, mountain lions, and snakes getting more press when it comes to dangers posed to hikers.

The most common mechanism behind fatal bee, hornet, and wasp stings is sudden-onset allergic reaction (within 10 minutes), or anaphylaxis, in hypersensitive individuals. The majority of fatal anaphylactic reactions are caused by upper airway constriction, resulting in an inability to breathe.

The medical evidence suggests that people with a history of systemic hypersensitivity to bee stings (dizziness, difficulty breathing) should consult their physicians about carrying self-injectable epinephrine (EpiPen). This can be a lifesaver if you're severely allergic to bee stings and are considering a long-distance hike.

For everyone, it's helpful to know how to avoid bees when hiking.

Smells. Bees are attracted to strong fragrances. Thus, it's important to avoid strong-smelling soaps, perfumes, or deodorants when in the wilderness, which is not a problem for most hikers.

Color. Pay attention to your clothing. Bees are known to become defensive around dark colors. If you have a history of severe reactions to bee stings, you may want to consider wearing light-colored clothing.

Flowers. Stay far away from areas where bees are collecting nectar from flowering plants.

Bananas. Avoid carrying bananas around areas where bees are present. This suggestion might *sound* bananas, but when a bee stings, it releases a pheromone that signals other bees to come and sting at the same site. This pheromone is similar to isopentyl acetate, which is found in bananas.

Mice

Mice are the bane of the AT shelter system. The shelters can make hiking the AT a truly ultralight and social experience, but many of them are overrun with mice, particularly the more popular shelters that are used by day and section hikers as well as long-distance hikers. On my southbound AT thru-hike, I found that the shelter mouse problem was at its worst from southwest Virginia through Georgia. This may have been because of the time of year since, like bears getting ready to hibernate, mice also need to store food in preparation for the winter. I remember lying awake one night watching the mice line up one-by-one in the shelter rafters, running a well-rehearsed route around the entire shelter looking for stray scraps. One even scurried over my head as I was sound asleep. Mice will do anything to get at even the smallest amount of food, and I've known many a hiker to wake up in the morning to find a hole chewed through a backpack.

Keeping mice from being a problem on a hike is fairly straightforward, and many of the strategies used to keep bears away from food also work on mice.

Use a bear canister. Easy and simple. Put all food and food scraps in the canister, seal it, place it away from the sleeping area, and rest easy. Mice can't chew through canisters. Don't forget to put away toothpaste, toothbrush, or anything else that might be mistaken as food.

Hang your food. Hanging food by the traditional method of tying it to a high tree branch generally prevents mice from getting to food. Do not hang food in this manner if you are camping in an area with problem bears (see pages 162 to 163). For AT shelter-goers who are disinclined to hang their food at all (and there are many of you), many AT shelters are rigged with homemade mouse ropes.

> Mouse ropes are ropes strung from the rafters of a shelter with an object such as an empty tuna can tied at the end. A food bag can be tied below the tuna can. The theory is that a mouse may be able to sneak down the rope, but cannot crawl around the can. These work pretty well on mice, but a hungry bear would have no problem at all . . .

Double- and triple-check backpacks. All it takes is a stray piece of food for a mouse to rip a hole through even the toughest backpack.

Sleep away from shelters. Granted, if you want to be around people from time to time or rely on shelters for, well, shelter, this isn't an option. But for those with a low tolerance for mice, you may want to eat and socialize at shelters, but sleep somewhere else.

Carry mousetraps. This is kind of a joke, but I met a guy outside of Damascus, Virginia, who did just this. (Naturally, we called him "Mousetrap.") I spent a few nights in shelters with Mousetrap and each night, at some wee morning hour we would all hear a *snap* and a faint *squeak*. Mousetrap would rouse himself, rub his eyes, turn on his headlamp, grab the trap, and toss the mouse out behind the shelter. Sometimes the mouse would not quite be dead and then Mousetrap would grab a rock and finish the job. It made for a few interesting evenings to say the least.

Ants

Ants are on the opposite end of the size spectrum from bears, but can be just as much of a nuisance. Someone once joked to me that instead of the bear, the California state flag should proudly display a giant ant. Anyone who has spent a significant amount of time on the PCT understands that long-distance hikers are guests in a world of ants. That said, unlike bears, there's really no way to manage ants. We just have to deal with them and adapt to their presence. The best advice, then, is to be mindful of campsite location, particularly when cowboy camping. Ants are forever out exploring their surroundings and will be especially curious of that lump inside a sleeping bag that has crash-landed outside their front door. I

Cowboy camping means camping without a shelter.

remember hiking just south of Tehachapi, California, one evening where I had chosen a bit of sandy, flat ground behind a bush to camp, just under a giant wind turbine. I had casually noticed the ants scurrying about at the campsite but was too tired and too used to seeing ants to care. I laid down my tarp and threw my sleeping bag on top to cowboy camp. No sooner had I dozed off to sleep when the first ant got inside my sleeping bag. All night I felt the little guys marching around my legs inside my bag, exploring every inch. Periodically, I would stand up, shake out my sleeping bag, scrutinize it with a headlamp for remaining ants, then move a few feet, and go back to sleep. I was getting no sleep this way. Finally, around midnight, I deployed my bivy and got inside of it, being very careful to make sure all ants were out of my bag and none had snuck inside. On other occasions, ants have ruined naps, crawled on food, and pretty much gotten on my nerves. Distance hikers, particularly those traveling along the sandy soil of the PCT in California, need to deal with ants as a fact of life. Nothing is out of their reach, and every ant is curious. I've found that it's just best to find a space where there are no ants and be happy if they don't find me eventually.

Fire ants

Fire ants deserve special mention. Two species, the black and red invasive fire ant, are thought to have been introduced in the United States aboard cargo ships from South America during the early and mid-twentieth century. Black invasive fire ants are currently considered contained to Alabama and Mississippi. The red invasive fire ant, on the other hand, has been an aggressive colonizer and has spread through much of eastern Texas and the American southeast. The ant is expected to eventually colonize western Texas, southern New Mexico and Arizona, as well as most of California and portions of southeast Virginia. Since these species of stinging ants are from the same evolutionary order as bees, hornets, and wasps, those who are severely allergic to bee, hornet, or wasp stings will also be severely allergic to the sting of a fire ant and should take extra precaution to avoid sleeping where ants are especially active.

Snakes, Spiders, and Scorpions

The chance of being fatally wounded by a snake or spider while hiking is exceedingly rare. A 2005 study from the University of North Carolina looked at deaths due to animal attacks in the United States from 1991 to 2001. The data from the study indicated that, on average, venomous snakes and spiders kill about 12 people annually in the entire United States. Scorpion stings are far more rare and accounted for only 5 deaths over the 10-year study period. Data also indicate that most deaths due to snakes, spiders, and scorpions occur in the south.

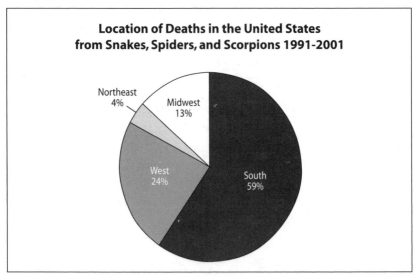

Source: Langley RL. 2005. *Animal-related fatalities in the United States—an update.* Wilderness and Environmental Medicine. *16:67–74.*

Considering the above numbers, worrying about snake and spider bites and scorpion stings while hiking in the United States should occupy a small portion of the distance hiker's brain. Nonetheless, getting bitten, seriously or not, is an unpleasant experience, and trying to gauge whether or not a wound inflicted by a snake, spider, or scorpion is serious is beyond the skill level of most hikers. Common-sense precautions will ensure that the microscopic risk of serious injury from a snake, spider, or scorpion stays low.

Look first. Don't reach blindly into spaces when you're not certain what lies inside. Snakes, spiders, and scorpions are not social animals and will scurry away when approached unless they feel threatened. An attack resulting in a bite is usually a last resort for most animals.

Music. In areas where rattlesnakes are common, avoid using headphones to listen to music. Many PCT hikers encounter rattlesnakes along the southern California section, sometimes right on the trail. Rattlesnakes are most active during the spring months, when they are hungry after hibernation. Thankfully, rattlesnakes usually use their rattle to warn oncoming hikers that they are encroaching.

> Lizards are a big part of the rattlesnake's diet, and as any PCT hiker can attest, lizards are plentiful in the sandy soils of southern California.

The sound is unmistakable, but if you can't hear the rattle because you're jamming along to Snoop Dogg, you put yourself at risk. Perhaps you could listen with low volume or one ear bud off. If you do happen to spot a rattlesnake on the trail, respect the snake and give it a wide berth. If it doesn't slither away, walk off the trail and make a large circle to get around it.

On the rare occasion a bite is sustained, there's not much that can be done while on the trail. If you suspect you've been bitten by a venomous spider or snake, the best thing to do is to immediately head for civilization and seek medical attention. Most bites from venomous snakes and spiders take time to inflict serious harm on the adult human body, so evacuation from the trail is the best choice.

Recent evidence has cast doubt on the efficacy of snakebite kits, which use a suction device to extract venom. Again, the best thing to do if you are bitten is to seek medical attention as soon as possible.

Ticks

Tick bites affect hikers each year, sometimes with permanent consequences. Deer ticks are responsible for the spread of Lyme disease, a bacterial infection that, if left untreated, can cause permanent damage to the circulatory,

Of the 27 AT finishers who took the 2011 survey, 17 (63 percent) reported being bitten by a tick. Five sought medical attention and four experienced symptoms:

- "Very sick, soreness, shakes, sweats, and dizzy."
- "Circular rash, flulike tiredness and chills."
- "Excessive fatigue, body aches, lack of appetite."

nervous, and musculoskeletal systems. Deer ticks are particularly problematic because they are so small and their bites are not always felt because the tick can release an anesthetic substance during the bite. You may not know that a tick bite has actually occurred until you see the bite or the tick has swollen to a visible size. Ticks are especially problematic in the northeastern and mid-Atlantic United States. It's not always easy to avoid bites, but here are some guidelines that will hopefully reduce the chances of a bite:

Cover up. Wearing long-sleeved shirts and leggings makes it hard for the tick to get to your skin. If the clothing is light-colored, then seeing a tick is easier. When it's hot out, though, wearing such clothing can be uncomfortable.

Use insect repellant. A repellant with DEET or permethrin works on ticks as well as mosquitoes and black flies. Be sure the repellant label says it works on ticks and note how long a repellant is effective before reapplication is required.

In areas like New England and the mid-Atlantic where Lyme disease–carrying ticks can be a problem, make frequent tick checks. Ticks land on their victim when the victim brushes by whatever blade of grass or leaf the tick happens to be sitting on. This is the *only* way ticks can get to their victim. It is unclear if ticks are able to intentionally fall from a high branch. Ticks certainly don't jump or fly, as is commonly perceived. Check for ticks whenever walking through tall grass or a brushy, overgrown section of trail.

If you find that a tick has penetrated your defenses and attached to you, make sure you remove it as soon as possible. Don't worry about leav-

Anatomy of a tick check: When checking for ticks, I usually start on my shoes, carefully checking the space between my socks and the shoe. From here I straighten my socks and move up my legs, looking and feeling for tiny black spots or something in motion. After a quick check of my groin area I'm on to my torso, giving special attention to my armpits. Finally, I run my hands through my hair, behind my ears, and along the base of my scalp. The whole process takes less than a minute and I've tossed away many ticks using this method.

ing behind the mouthparts or trying to remove it in a certain way. When it comes to transmission of *Borrelia burgdorferi*, the bacteria that causes Lyme disease, the length of time a tick is attached is more important than the method by which it is removed. Lyme disease does not occur if a tick is attached for less than 24 hours. If you happen to be carrying tweezers, the best method is to get as close to the skin as possible, pinch the tick, and pull gently, but steadily. Without tweezers, just pull the tick off, doing your best to remove as much of the tick as possible. After you remove the tick, be sure to clean the area, using whatever materials you may be carrying. I carry a 1-ounce bottle of hand sanitizer that I use for this purpose. Keep the tick, if possible, in case it needs to be identified in the future. Over the ensuing month, monitor the bite area. You should immediately get off the trail and seek medical attention if you notice any of the following symptoms between three and thirty days following a tick bite:

1. A strange rash. Lyme disease rashes come in all sizes and shapes, not just bull's eyes.
2. Flulike symptoms such as unusual fatigue, chills, and cramps.
3. Painful, swollen joints. Of course, lots of hikers have sore joints, perhaps with a bit of swelling. This is par for the course. But pain and swelling due to Lyme will be timed in concert with a tick bite and might not resemble the familiar soreness of hiking. Northbound AT hikers who suddenly experience nontraumatic joint pain and swelling in the New England states should seek medical attention.

These are all telltale signs of Lyme disease. Treated early, Lyme disease will usually be harmless. If ignored, the consequences could be as bad as permanent disablement.

10

Finances

Whether we like it or not, money plays an important role in the likelihood of completing a long-distance hike. Simply put: If the money runs out, the hike is over.

It's unfortunate to have to unexpectedly quit a trail because of money, but it happens each year.

An often-heard mantra for estimating costs on a long-distance trail is "$1 per mile." This grossly underestimates the true cost of a longdistance hike for most people.

> **I**n the 2011 survey, 10 percent of AT and PCT hikers who did not finish cited finances as the most influential reason. One AT hiker wrote, "I got to Harpers Ferry with 11 dollars to my name, so I had to go home." Among finishers, 12 percent found dealing with finances to be the most challenging aspect of the trail.

Of the 85 thru-hikers who completed the 2011 survey, 72 percent spent more than $3,000 on the trail, which is considerably more dollars than miles for the PCT and the AT. Thru-hikers spent a surprisingly wide distribution of money while hiking in 2011. Interestingly, although a clear majority of hikers spent between $3,000 and $4,999, costs varied considerably, ranging from less than $1,000 to over $10,000.

If miles-per-day does not provide realistic guidance as to the financial cost of long-distance hiking, then what is the best way to plan? The short answer is that details count. To get a sense of how much a long-distance hike will cost, you'll need to make a few assumptions and do some math. A good way to plan finances is to look at costs in two categories: those associated with the actual hiking part of the trip, including town stops, and those associated with things that happen before and after the trip.

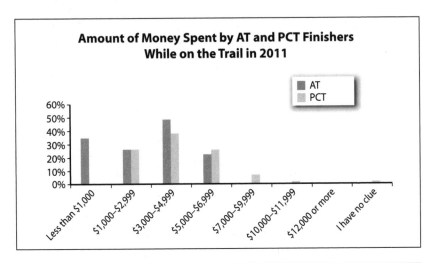

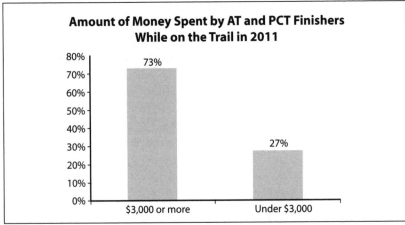

Eighty-four thru-hikers completed the survey. Reported costs do not include pre- and post-trail expenses or recurring expenses from home such as mortgage, rent, student loan interest, etc. Couples were asked to divide their costs by two to get a per-person cost.

Hiking Costs

Hiking costs fall into three main categories: trail food, town (shipping, motels, restaurants), and gear replacement and repair.

Trail food

Costs vary depending on dietary preferences. Eating on the cheap costs around $8 per day. Eating better might run closer to $15 per day.

Town

Town expenses can be huge and entirely depend on your need to hop in a shower, get into a comfy bed, and eat real food. If you're new to long-distance hiking or know you'll be craving comfort often, you'll want to budget on the high side for town expenses. Motels will probably cost you around $100 per night; hostels cost much less, anywhere from a donation to $15 or $20. Two meals in town cost around $30. Miscellaneous spending, perhaps $50. Shipping a bounce box is $15. All said and done, it's safe to say a full day in town can cost about $200, maybe $150 for thriftier folks or for each member of a couple. You'll need to put the numbers together and come up with your own scenarios.

Gear

Budget around $500 for replacement and repair if your gear is high quality. Most of this will be spent on periodic replacement of your footwear. Budget $1,000 if you bought your gear on the cheap.

Off-Trail Costs

Off-trail costs fall into four broad categories: preparation, transportation, monthly financial commitments, and relocation.

Preparation

These costs are mostly associated with purchasing gear for your trip. If you're buying all new high-quality gear, plan on spending between $2,000 and $3,000. Budget less if you are purchasing secondhand gear, already have some of your own gear, or are sharing gear with a partner.

> Transportation can also be time-consuming. After attending a wedding, my wife and I needed to get from New York to Lemhi, Idaho, to resume hiking the CDT. This route involved a train, two flights, a cab ride, and eight hitches.

Transportation

Getting to or from the trail can range from nothing for the highly resourceful to over $500 for a train or airplane ride. It's not unusual for hikers to take a little time off the trail to get to weddings, see family, and so on, so make sure to include these costs.

Monthly financial commitments

Expenses here include, but are not limited to, student loans, car payments, mortgage or rent, child support or alimony, cell phone, and credit card.

Relocation costs

Lastly, if you are not retired or returning to school, consider how much it will cost to get back into the work force or find a new place to live. These costs can be minor or huge, depending individual circumstances.

Total it all up. Long-distance hiking is a simple pursuit, but it ain't cheap! Go ahead and pat yourself on the back anyway. You've taken a big step toward getting yourself ready for a successful hike. For additional help with financial planning, try using the handy planner on page 179.

Simple Financial Planner for Long-Distance Hiking

On Trail

	Best Case	Worst Case
Daily Food Cost		
Days of Hiking		
SUBTOTAL A:		
Cost per Town Stop		
Number of Town Stops		
SUBTOTAL B:		
Gear Replacement and Repair		
ON-TRAIL TOTAL:		

Off Trail

	Best Case	Worst Case
Gear Purchases		
Transportation		
Relocation Costs		
Monthly Obligations		
Months on Trail		
SUBTOTAL:		
OFF-TRAIL TOTAL:		

11

Partners

Hiking with a dedicated partner is a much different experience than hiking solo because partners hiking presents a unique set of challenges not encountered in solo hiking. My own experience with having a partner has varied from chance meetings with one or a few other hikers along the way to hiking with a dedicated partner for an entire journey.

After living and working overseas, my wife, April, and I decided to come back to the United States and hike the CDT in 2010. Even though this was her first long-distance hike, I felt confident that my experience thru-hiking the AT and PCT would accelerate her learning curve and that we'd be making good miles within a few weeks. This turned out to be overconfidence on my part as we encountered a few obstacles along the way that affected our ability to finish the trail that year. One was a knee injury. Through the grind of clearing tall passes in Glacier National Park, Montana, April's knees and ankles began to get progressively more painful. Despite our best efforts, including several breaks from the trail, April's pain never seemed to get much better. She hadn't done much hiking at all in the past, so long-distance backpacking was truly a novel experience for her body, and we probably should have started out over less steep terrain before tackling Glacier.

The other obstacle, one that probably had a greater effect on the trip, was that we found out we had different styles of hiking. We both enjoy the experience of a long journey, but she likes to linger in places and take her time and I like to be up on my feet moving most of the time. This basic difference in style and approach made for a number of tense moments, and we almost broke off the journey a few times due to these basic differences. We ended up hiking only the Montana section that year, and looking back, we both agree that the experience was positive. We're excited about our next trip back to the CDT, when we will have a combined style that's all our own with some agreed-upon expectations for what we want to get out of the trip. For us, the most important thing is to have a shared, enjoyable, and relaxing experience. To this end, we both compromise certain aspects of our own individual styles of hiking.

Hiking with a partner or as a couple is not an unusual way to thru-hike. In fact, 44 percent of thru-hikers who took the 2011 survey reported hiking the trail with the same partner for more than 75 percent of the way. Not surprisingly, most identified the opportunity to share an experience as what they liked best about hiking with a partner.

What Did You Like the Most about Hiking with a Partner?

- Companionship, partner in decision making.
- My wife.
- Share weight of tent and gear.
- Friendship and sharing the experience with someone.
- It's always nice to have someone to share an experience with.
- Security and comfort of having another person near in case "sh** hit the fan," not to mention a good laugh goes many a mile on the trail.
- Mutual encouragement and entertainment.
- Loved hiking with my partner. Made it fun to experience all those places and moments with someone. Someone to talk to and help you when you're down or through challenges.
- Always having someone to share the experience with, whether it was a good experience or a bad one, there was someone there to help you through it or someone to enjoy it with.
- She kept a regular blog, so my family didn't have to worry about me. In general having shared responsibilities was great.
- Someone to talk to, laugh with during the day. Security . . . nice to know someone is close by.
- She has a wonderful attitude and hiking ability to match.
- Fun to share the experience.
- Fun times, someone to hang out with at camp, and someone to share memories with.
- Division of labor, moral support, safety during river crossings and in snowy traverses, teamwork during route finding.
- It was nice to have someone who really knew and understood me to support me through the challenging days.

- It was nice to have someone there so I didn't have to go at it alone. The scary sections weren't as scary and there was someone there who remembered the same experiences as you.
- To have someone to share experiences with, to have someone to talk to and someone to help keeping up the spirit and support when you're down.
- There was always someone there to support you (physically, mentally, even financially). You never know when you will need the help of another person.
- It was nice to have someone helping when times got tough and scary (river crossings, crazy weather, getting lost in snow).
- Less weight, support for river crossings and snow travel, and company.
- He's my best friend, and I got to do everything with him.
- Having someone to share the experience with.
- Someone to face challenges with (e.g. creek crossings).
- Loyal.
- Just having someone I knew and that knew me as a person before the trail and could think back on old memories of home and friends.
- Camaraderie and safety in numbers. Help in orienteering.
- Having a companion that knew my limits and was willing to adapt to them, and vise versa with him. It was nice having someone with you if you had to make a difficult decision; I never had to worry about being "left behind."
- Encouragement, and the need to keep moving forward together. Also sharing hotel rooms and groceries at times. And someone that you care about to share experiences with.
- I hiked with my girlfriend of eight years. She thinks like me and she is my best friend, and when I didn't want to keep going she was my rock.
- Easy going.
- I always had someone to count on who wouldn't leave me because we hiked at different paces. If I got lost, I didn't have to sleep alone and lost. Two pairs of eyes were good for finding trail in the snow.
- Great company; met her on the trail and now we're living together. Amazing!
- I liked to have someone there to experience it with. We hiked the whole thing together. We were a couple that stayed a couple before and after. I could depend on him for anything. He helped when one

of my muscles gave out outside of Wrightwood. He carried all the extra weight that was causing me pain. We also pushed each other every day. We were each other's motivational speakers.

- Companionship.
- Not having to worry about being alone, always having someone to hitch with and share motel rooms with.
- Sharing the experience with someone close to me.
- Spending lots of quality time with my best friend.

Some of the more challenging aspects of partners hiking included choice making, especially around pace and style.

What Did You Find Most Challenging about Hiking with a Partner?

- Not being able to hike on my own schedule.
- Different paces.
- Keeping the same pace.
- Had to compromise on many things (mileage, town stops). Luckily, we usually were able to listen to each other and work together
- Decision making.
- Varying hiking styles (although that's the beauty of choosing a partner—styles are usually similar). Most challenging aspect was probably different desires and agendas while resupplying in town.
- Sometimes we could get a little short with each other, but rarely.
- Finding a good rhythm. Getting up and going at the same time.
- If I was having a bad day, my anger was directed only at my partner because that's who was there all the time. A partner sees the best in you, but also the worst, and the trail has the ability to bring out both.
- Adjusting my pace or goals for the day according to the needs of my partner.
- My partner was faster than me, so it was challenging to feel like I had to "keep up" some of the times, especially on snowy terrain.
- Sharing decisions about where and when to stop.
- Harder to make certain choices.
- Wanting to hike at different paces, i.e. when to take zero days, how many miles to hike in a day, etc. We usually wouldn't hike together during the day, but ended up at the same camp.
- If somebody was having a bad day (not very often).

- When we would both get tired and hungry and get a bit irritable at the end of the day. It's not like you can just hike away, it's your hiking partner. But you want to and the freedom that the trail provides tells you that you could if you really wanted to.
- I couldn't have my own schedule of when to take breaks, how long to stay in town, hiking speed, etc. Everything had to be a compromise when sometimes I just wanted things on my own schedule. Also, I felt that I missed out on being alone in nature. Thought it's amazing to be able to share certain things, sometimes it's nice to have the experience all to yourself, the independence and aloneness of being alone. Also, petty bickering and arguing suck when you're stuck with the same person in the wilderness and can't get away.
- The social aspects of sharing ALL your time for five months with one single person with little or no mental resources.
- We got on each other's nerves ALL THE TIME! But it became part of our relationship and at least we could laugh the constant bickering off.
- Nothing.
- Conflicting opinions on how far to go every day.
- Different speeds.
- Hiking with a girlfriend can be tough. Couples really have to be on the same page when planning a thru-hike.
- Learning to compromise and share decision making—where to camp, what pace to hike at, what to eat for dinner . . .
- Pacing.
- Knowing when to give space and when to engage in conversation.
- Differing paces and levels of urgency with regard to mileage achieved on a given day.
- Differences in personality.
- Conflicting morals.
- He was pessimistic some days and didn't get along with one of the other guys that we started hiking with.
- I was always with her. Didn't get much alone time.
- n/a.
- I needed alone time more often than I got it.
- Saying goodbye at the end for a month.
- When we were starving in the High Sierra from not bringing enough, we fought every day, all day long. It was really stressful.

We often fought, but it was really hard to be together when we were both starving to death. We each lost 20 pounds that week. He never fully recovered from that.

- Nothing too challenging.
- We both had to compromise a lot about what we wanted in terms of schedule/pace. And inevitably, you get sick of anyone you're around that much.
- Compromising on pace differences.
- Staying positive when my partner was struggling with trail challenges.

There are some common themes that come up when hiking with a dedicated partner. If you're thinking of heading out on a long-distance hike with a special someone or a good friend, and you're committing to hiking with each other, here are some important things to plan for that might reduce some (but not all) of the stress of the journey.

Set Expectations

Hopefully both partners know that long-distance hiking entails living in a small tent; sleeping on the ground; getting sweaty; being cold, tired, and hungry; smelling bad; swatting mosquitoes; and taking an occasional shower. If this is a surprise to anyone in the partnership, then you have some basics to cover before getting into the specifics about partner dynamics. Basics aside, perhaps the most important thing that partners need to do before setting foot on the trail is to mutually agree upon the expectations. "Expectations" can mean a number of things, but at the minimum, prospective partners should discuss the following topics:

- Why are we hiking this trail?
- What do we want to get out of the experience?
- Are we committed to finishing? If so, is finishing an absolute priority or will we be satisfied to not finish if it means having a better shared experience?
- Are we going to stay together the whole time or is this going to be more of an informal partnership?
- What happens when one of us gets injured and needs to take time off or quit?

Acknowledge Gaps in Fitness and Experience

Partners need to be frank with each other about a gap in experience level or general fitness. The less fit or less experienced partner will struggle to keep up if the other partner is not able to compromise and accommodate. This can cause feelings of resentment and regret from both partners if you don't discuss it ahead of time. Personally, I feel as though the more experienced or fit partner has a duty to bring up the topic, since the other partner is liable to suffer silently rather than ask the more experienced or fit partner to slow down. If it's possible, try to take a practice hike before the long-distance hike to generate a conversation about pace and fitness levels.

If paces don't match on the trail, and this begins to affect the happiness of one or both partners, here are a few ideas to keep the peace:

- The slower partner gets head starts by leaving 10 to 15 minutes earlier from camp or after breaks, stopping at a time or location you agreed upon. This allows both hikers to hike at their own pace for parts of the day.
- During level ground or downhill hiking, the slower partner leads. During uphill climbs, the faster partner leads, stopping at the top or after a predetermined period of time.

For these methods to work, both partners should be proficient at navigating and the way should be clear, without ambiguities or questionable turns. If this is not the case, partners should ignore the first tip and modify the second so that they remain within earshot of one another. Both partners should have food and water on board.

The other important thing to consider, when you have a significant experience gap between partners, is that the less experienced partner is going through a major learning process. It is up to the more experienced partner to be a patient teacher. There's no sense in getting impatient or angry when your partner doesn't stuff down his sleeping bag well, fumbles with the map, makes a wrong turn, complains about aches and pains, or doesn't get out of camp fast enough.

The experienced partner should remember his first time on a long trip in order to keep perspective. Use these opportunities to teach and show in order to build your partner's capacity to be an equal partner. Allow your partner to take the lead on things that you have always done.

The less experienced partner should be open to learning things he may not feel comfortable with initially. Practice taking the lead on different camp chores or navigating for a day.

Be Honest about Needing Alone Time

Time spent solo in nature can be an intensely spiritual and gratifying experience. Although being in a dedicated partnership means another person is close by throughout the journey, it doesn't mean that you never have a chance to enjoy the wilderness in solitude. Alone time in a partnership can be in the form of hiking ahead or behind for a while or staying up while the other is asleep. On the PCT, my friends Optimist and Stopwatch had a system in place when one wanted to get ahead of the other to have alone time. The person hiking ahead agreed to stop to wait for the other at a landmark or after a certain period of time. On the CDT, my wife and I had a less formal arrangement. "Please don't wait for me," usually meant that she wanted to be alone for a while.

What's important is that dedicated partners are each able to communicate his or her need for alone time without the other taking offense. It is helpful for each person in a partnership to reflect on how important alone time is to him or her. If you don't discuss this, tempers and egos may flare, threatening the harmony of the partnership.

A final reflection: I've always leaned toward solo hiking over hiking with a partner. My 2002 and 2007 thru-hikes of the AT and PCT were both done solo with periodic, but uncommitted partnerships along the way. Even though I have vivid memories and lots of pictures from both trips, after hiking with my wife along the Montana section of the CDT in 2010 I now prefer hiking with a partner. She and I reflect back quite a bit on the people and places we both got to experience. If either of us ever wants to relive part of our journey, we only need to pull up some pictures, read our old blogs, or laugh together over a meal. It's a level of reflection that I've never gotten from a solo trip. We're both looking forward to getting back out on the CDT in years to come.

Appendix

**Nutritional Content of
Common Backpacking Foods**

Food	Quantity	Weight (g)	Total Calories	Total Carbs	Total Fat	Calorie Density (cal/g)
Amazing Grass Green Superfood: Berry Whole Energy Bar	1 bar	60	210	35	8	3.5
Amazing Grass Green Superfood: Chocolate Peanut Butter Protein Bar	1 bar	63	270	28	14	4.3
Amazing Grass Green Superfood: Chocolate Whole Energy Bar	1 bar	60	230	37	9	3.8
Amazing Grass Green Superfood: Whole Food Energy Bar	1 bar	60	210	36	8	3.5
Backpacker's Pantry: Beef Stroganoff	2-serving pouch	187	520	60	20	2.8
Backpacker's Pantry: Cajun Style Rice and Chicken	2-serving pouch	182	620	112	4	3.4
Backpacker's Pantry: Chana Masala	2-serving pouch	250	740	162	3	3.0
Backpacker's Pantry: Chicken Cashew Curry	2-serving pouch	147	580	88	12	3.9
Backpacker's Pantry: Chicken Vindaloo	2-serving pouch	150	520	92	6	3.5
Backpacker's Pantry: Jamaican Jerk Rice with Chicken	2-serving pouch	179	620	116	0	3.5
Backpacker's Pantry: Katmandu Curry	2-serving pouch	187	660	128	3	3.5
Backpacker's Pantry: Kung Pao Rice w/ Chicken	2-serving pouch	200	740	114	14	3.7
Backpacker's Pantry: Organic Black Bean Chili Pie	1-serving pouch	130	550	71	23	4.2
Backpacker's Pantry: Organic Tofu Pesto	1-serving pouch	99	260	27	10	2.6
Backpacker's Pantry: Pad See You with Chicken	2-serving pouch	187	740	126	14	4.0
Backpacker's Pantry: Pad Thai	2-serving pouch	228	920	128	36	4.0
Backpacker's Pantry: Yakisoba Noodles	1-serving pouch	116	420	63	14	3.6
Bonk Breaker: Almond Butter and Honey	1 bar	62	255	37	9	4.1
Carnation Instant Breakfast	1 packet	36	130	27	0	3.6
Cheerios	1 box	252	900	180	18	3.6

Food	Quantity	Weight (g)	Total Calories	Total Carbs	Total Fat	Calorie Density (cal/g)
Cheese, mozarella (whole milk)	8 oz (226 g) package	226	640	8	48	2.8
Cheese, sharp cheddar	8 oz (226 g) package	226	720	0	48	3.2
Cheetos	1 bag	276	1600	150	100	5.8
Chow Mein (chicken)	1 box	113	540	64	28	4.8
Cinnamon Toast Crunch	1 box	362	1430	275	33	4.0
Clif Bar: Black Cherry Almond	1 bar	68	240	44	5	3.5
Clif Bar: Carrot Cake	1 bar	68	240	45	5	3.5
Clif Bar: Chocolate Almond Fudge	1 bar	68	240	42	6	3.5
Clif Bar: Chocolate Blueberry Crisp	1 bar	68	240	43	5	3.5
Clif Bar: Chocolate Chip	1 bar	68	240	44	5	3.5
Clif Bar: Chocolate Chip Peanut Crunch	1 bar	68	240	41	7	3.5
Clif Bar: White Chocolate Macadamia Nut	1 bar	68	250	42	7	3.7
Clif Luna Bar: Chocolate Dipped Coconut	1 bar	48	190	25	7	4.0
Clif Luna Bar: Cookies n Cream Delight	1 bar	48	180	28	5	3.8
Clif Luna Bar: Lemon Zest	1 bar	48	180	27	5	3.8
Clif Luna Bar: S'mores	1 bar	48	180	27	5	3.8
Clif Shot Energy Gel	1 pouch	34	100	24	2	2.9
Coffee, Iced, Starbucks Via	1 packet	26	100	24	0	2.6
Couscous	1 box	284	990	207	5	3.5
Cracklin' Oat Bran	1 box	482	2000	350	70	4.1

Food	Quantity	Weight (g)	Total Calories	Total Carbs	Total Fat	Calorie Density (cal/g)
Devil Dog	1 cake	45	170	26	7	3.8
Doritos Cool Ranch	1 bag	326	1800	216	96	5.5
Fritos Original	1 bag	397	2240	224	140	5.6
Fruity Pebbles	1 box	311	1320	276	12	4.2
Granola, Bear Naked Banana	1 bag	340	1540	198	77	4.5
Granola, Bear Naked Fruit and Nut	1 bag	340	1540	198	77	4.5
Granola, Bear Naked Maple Pecan	1 bag	340	1430	242	44	4.2
Granola, Bear Naked Peak Protein	1 bag	340	1540	165	77	4.5
Grape Nuts	1 box	680	2400	576	12	3.5
Gu Energy Gel	1 pouch	31	100	25	2	3.2
Hershey's Milk Chocolate Bar	1 bar	43	210	26	13	4.9
Hostess Cup Cake	1 cake	50	180	29	7	3.6
Hot Cocoa (from mix)	1 envelope	21	90	16	2	4.3
Hot Pocket (pepperoni pizza)	1 hot pocket	127	680	74	34	5.4
Idahoan Potatoes: Buttery Golden	1 pouch	116	440	84	12	3.8
Idahoan Potatoes: Loaded Baked	1 pouch	113	440	80	10	3.9
Instant Oatmeal, Quaker, Apples and Cinnamon	1 packet	35	130	27	2	3.7
Instant Oatmeal, Quaker, Maple Brown Sugar	1 packet	43	160	32	3	3.7
Jack Link's Beef Jerky: Original Recipe	1 pouch	92	240	9	3	2.6
Jell-O Instant Pudding	1 box	96	400	92	0	4.2

Food	Quantity	Weight (g)	Total Calories	Total Carbs	Total Fat	Calorie Density (cal/g)
Jell-O No Bake Cheesecake	1 box	314	1320	252	30	4.2
Justin's Peanut Butter: Honey Peanut	1 pouch	33	190	17	8	5.8
Kashi Go Lean Crunch	1 box	425	1520	296	24	3.6
KIND Fruit and Nut: Apple Cinnamon and Pecan	1 bar	40	170	16	11	4.3
Kix	1 box	340	1210	275	11	3.6
Knorr Pasta Sides: Alfredo	1 pouch	124	440	72	9	3.5
Knorr Rice Sides: Chicken Flavor	1 pouch	158	600	118	6	3.8
Lay's Baked	1 bag	255	1080	207	18	4.2
Lay's Classic Chips	1 bag	298	1760	165	110	5.9
Lenders Bagels (plain)	1 bag	340	840	174	3	2.5
Lipton cup-a-soup mix (chicken noodle)	1 box	51	200	32	4	3.9
Lucky Charms	1 box	326	1320	264	12	4.0
Mac and Cheese, Annie's White Cheddar	1 box	170	675	118	10	4.0
Mac and Cheese, Kraft Homestyle	1 pouch	357	1120	164	32	3.1
Mac and Cheese, Kraft Regular	1 box	206	650	118	9	3.2
Macaroni, elbow	1 box	454	1600	328	8	3.5
Marchuan Instant Lunch (chicken)	1 container	64	290	38	12	4.5
Mary Jane's Farm: Curried Lentil Bisque	1 pouch	102	390	56	8	3.8
Mary Jane's Farm: Cheesy B.N.T.	1 pouch	122	465	65	15	3.8
Mary Jane's Farm: Cheesy Noodle Casserole	1 pouch	122	465	63	15	3.8

Food	Quantity	Weight (g)	Total Calories	Total Carbs	Total Fat	Calorie Density (cal/g)
Mary Jane's Farm: Chili Mac	1 pouch	139	525	75	14	3.8
Mary Jane's Farm: Kettle Chili	1 pouch	94	345	59	3	3.7
Mary Jane's Farm: Organic Wild Forest Mushroom Couscous	1 pouch	108	420	71	7	3.9
Mary Jane's Farm: Shepherd's Meat Pie	1 pouch	113	375	54	9	3.3
Milk, dry, Nestle Nido	1 can	360	1680	132	96	4.7
Mountain House: Buffalo Style Chicken (Wrap)	1-serving pouch	114	390	3	15	3.4
Mountain House: Beef Stew	2-serving pouch	122	500	60	18	4.1
Mountain House: Beef Stroganoff	2-serving pouch	136	620	72	24	4.6
Mountain House: Beef Stroganoff	Pro Pack	115	520	62	20	4.5
Mountain House: Breakfast Skillet (Wrap)	1-serving pouch	134	680	52	42	5.1
Mountain House: Chicken a la King Noodles	2-serving pouch	180	780	80	28	4.3
Mountain House: Chicken Salad (Wrap)	4-serving pouch	116	520	16	20	4.5
Mountain House: Chili Mac with Beef	2-serving pouch	136	580	78	16	4.3
Mountain House: Chili Mac with Beef	Pro Pack	115	500	67	14	4.3
Mountain House: Granola with Blueberries	1-serving pouch	113	500	71	19	4.4
Mountain House: Lasagna with Meat and Sauce	2-serving pouch	136	600	68	22	4.4
Mountain House: Pasta Primavera	2-serving pouch	136	520	82	14	3.8
Mountain House: Pasta Primavera	Pro Pack	115	440	71	12	3.8
Mountain House: Scrambled Eggs with Bacon	1-serving pouch	64	320	12	19	5.0
Mountain House: Sweet and Sour Pork with Rice	2-serving pouch	173	560	84	18	3.2

Food	Quantity	Weight (g)	Total Calories	Total Carbs	Total Fat	Calorie Density (cal/g)
Natural High: Cheese Enchilada Ranchero	2-serving pouch	177	840	104	34	4.7
Natural High: Chicken Pot Pie with Mashed Potatoes	2-serving pouch	170	560	98	12	3.3
Natural High: Homestyle Turkey with Mashed Potatoes	2-serving pouch	149	500	86	7	3.4
Natural High: Honey Lime Chicken	2-serving pouch	163	600	160	3	3.7
Natural High: Kung Pao Shrimp	2-serving pouch	135	440	88	3	3.3
Natural High: Spicy Sausage Pasta	2-serving pouch	142	620	76	22	4.4
Nature's Plus Siru-Teen: chocolate	1 pouch	28	96	10	0	3.4
Nature's Plus Siru-Teen: strawberry/vanilla/banana	1 pouch	34	99	11	0	2.9
Nutty Bar	2 bars	57	310	33	18	5.4
Odwalla: Chewy Nut	1 bar	45	220	22	11	4.9
Odwalla: Chocolate Chip Peanut	1 bar	56	230	33	8	4.1
Odwalla: Choco-walla	1 bar	56	210	39	5	3.8
Odwalla: Original Super Protein	1 bar	56	210	30	5	3.8
Odwalla: Strawberry Pomegranite Superfood	1 bar	56	200	42	2	3.6
Orzo, organic	1 box	454	1600	336	8	3.5
Pasta, angel hair	14.5 oz box	411	1470	266	14	3.6
Peanut butter, chunky	2 tablespoons	32	180	8	15	5.6
Pecans, chopped	1 bag	64	420	8	44	6.6
Pepperoni	6 oz (170 g) bag	170	780	0	72	4.6
Peter Rabbit Organics: Pea/Spinach/Apple	1 pouch	125	90	20	1	0.7

Food	Quantity	Weight (g)	Total Calories	Total Carbs	Total Fat	Calorie Density (cal/g)
Polenta, instant	1 box	260	850	204	0	3.3
Pop Tart: Frosted Strawberry	1 tart	52	200	38	5	3.8
Power Bar Energy Gel Blasts	1 bag	60	195	45	0	3.3
Pretzels, Rold Gold Tiny Twists	1 bag	454	1760	368	16	3.9
Pro Bar Halo: S'Mores	1 bar	37	150	25	5	4.1
Pro Bar: Apple Cinnamon Crunch	1 bar	85	370	49	18	4.4
Pro Bar: Art's Original Blend	1 bar	85	370	48	18	4.4
Pro Bar: Cran Lemon Twister	1 bar	85	360	49	16	4.2
Pro Bar: Koka Moka	1 bar	85	360	47	18	4.2
Pro Bar: Old School PB&J	1 bar	85	370	48	17	4.4
Pro Bar: Superfood Slam	1 bar	85	380	46	19	4.5
Quinoa	1 bag	340	1190	210	21	3.5
Raisin Bran	1 box	567	1710	414	9	3.0
Raisins	1 box	255	780	186	0	3.1
Ramen noodles (chicken)	1 pack	85	380	52	14	4.5
Red Beans and Rice	1 box	227	760	160	0	3.3
Rice Cakes	1 bag	127	490	98	0	3.9
Rice Pilaf, instant	1 box	172	570	129	2	3.3
Rice Pilaf, instant	1 pouch	250	420	86	5	1.7
Rice, instant white	1 pouch	240	420	82	5	1.8

Food	Quantity	Weight (g)	Total Calories	Total Carbs	Total Fat	Calorie Density (cal/g)
Rice, instant, boil in bag	1 box	396	1520	344	0	3.8
Ruffles Original	1 bag	269	1600	150	100	5.9
Smartfood White Cheddar	1 bag	255	1440	126	90	5.6
Spaghetti (plain)	8 oz box	227	840	164	4	3.7
Stove Top: Chicken Flavor	1 box	170	660	126	6	3.9
Sun Chips Original	1 bag	298	1540	209	66	5.2
Sunflower Seeds: roasted, salted	7 oz (198 g) bag	198	1330	28	126	6.7
Thomas Everything Bagels	1 bag	567	1680	306	24	3.0
Tortillas (Tex's brand)	1 tortilla	66	199	35	4	3.0
Tostitos Bite Size Rounds	1 bag	369	1820	234	91	4.9
Tuna, Starkist Tuna Creation, Zesty Lemon Pepper	1 pouch	128	150	0	1	1.2
Tuna, Starkist Tuna Creations, Sweet and Spicy	1 pouch	128	175	10	1	1.4
Twinkie	1 cake	43	150	27	5	3.5
Walnuts, Shelled	1 bag	64	400	8	40	6.3
Yakisoba Noodles (cheddar cheese)	1 box	113	560	66	28	5.0
Yogurt Raisins	1 bag	227	1040	168	40	4.6

Bibliography

Chapter 3

Backer H and Hollowell J. Use of iodine for water disinfection: iodine toxicity and maximum recommended dose. *Environmental Health Perspectives.* 2000;108(8): 680–84.

Chlorine Disinfection. January 2008. Publication by the Center for Affordable Water and Sanitation Technology.

Clorox Regular Bleach Material Safety Data Sheet. Prepared August 2009.

Derlet RW, et al. Risk factors for coliform bacteria in backcountry lakes and streams in the Sierra Nevada mountains: a 5-year study. *Wilderness and Environmental Medicine.* 2008;19:82–90.

Derlet RW and Carlson JR. Coliform bacteria in Sierra Nevada wilderness lakes and streams: what is the impact of backpackers, pack animals, and cattle? *Wilderness and Environmental Medicine.* 2006;17(1):15–21.

Drinking Water Chlorination: A review of disinfection practices and issues. 2003. Posted on the Water Quality and Health Council website. Accessed at http://www.waterandhealth.org/drinkingwater/wp.html on February 27, 2012.

Mattison K, et al. Human norovirus in swine and cattle. *Emerging Infectious Diseases.* 2007;13:1184–88.

Methods for the Investigation and Prevention of Waterborne Disease Outbreaks. Published by The United States Environmental Protection Agency. September 1990.

Peipins LA, et al. A Norwalk-like virus outbreak on the Appalachian Trail. *Journal of Environmental Health.* 2002;64(9):18–23.

Rockwell, R. *Giardia lamblia* and Giardiasis, with particular attention paid to the Sierra Nevada. June 4, 2003. Accessed from http://www.ridgenet.net/~rockwell/Giardia.pdf on February 27, 2012.

Chapter 5

Anderson LS, Rebholz CM, White LF, Mitchell P, Curcio EP, Feldman JA, and Kahn JH. 2009. The impact of footwear and packweight on injury and illness among long-distance hikers. *Wilderness and Environmental Medicine.* 20:250–6.

Arya S. and Kulig K. 2010. Tendinopathy alters mechanical and material properties of the Achilles tendon. *Journal of Applied Physiology.* 108:670–75.

Barnes A, Wheat J, and Milner C. 2008. Association between foot type and tibial stress injuries: a systematic review. *British Journal of Sports Medicine.* 42:93–98.

Craig DI. 2008. Medial tibial stress syndrome: evidenced-based prevention. *Journal of Athletic Training.* 43(3):316–18.

Fields KB, Sykes JC, Walker KM, and Jackson JC. 2010. Prevention of running injuries. *Sports Medicine Reports.* 9(3):176–82.

Hamonko MT, McIntosh SE, Schimelpfenig T, and Leemon D. 2011. Injuries related to hiking with a pack during National Outdoor Leadership School courses: a risk factor analysis. *Wilderness and Environmental Medicine.* 22:2–6.

Kader D, Saxena A, Movin T, and Maffulli N. 2002. Achilles tendinopathy: some basic aspects of basic science and clinical management. *British Journal of Sports Medicine.* 36:239–49.

Landorf KB, Keenan AM, and Herbert RD. 2006. Effectiveness of foot orthoses to treat plantar fasciitis: a randomized trial. *Archives of Internal Medicine.* 166:1305–10.

Lee SY, McKeon P, and Hertel J. 2009. Does the use of orthoses improve self-reported pain and function measures in patients with plantar fasciitis? *Physical Therapy in Sport.* 10:12–18.

Mattila VM, Sillanpää PJ, Salo T, Laine HJ, Maenpää H, and Pihlajamäki H. 2010. Can orthotic insoles prevent lower limb overuse injuries? A randomized-controlled trial of 228 subjects. *Scandinavian Journal of Medicine and Science in Sports.* doi: 10.1111/j.1600-0838.2010.01116.x. [Epub ahead of print]

Peers KHE and Lysens RJJ. 2005. Patellar tendinopathy in athletes: current diagnostic and therapeutic recommendations. *Sports Medicine.* 35(1):71–87.

Reinking MF and Hayes AM. 2006. Intrinsic factors associated with exercise-related leg pain in collegiate cross-country runners. *Clinical Journal of Sports Medicine.* 16(1):10–14.

Riddle DL, Pulisic M, Pidcoe P, Johnson RE. 2003. Risk factors for plantar fasciitis: a matched case-controlled study. *Journal of Bone and Joint Surgery.* 85-A (5):872–77.

Tan SC and Chan O. 2008. Achilles and patellar tendinopathy: current understanding of pathophysiology and management. *Disability and Rehabilitation.* 30(20-22):1608–15.

Thacker SB, Gilchrist J, Stroup DF, and Kimsey CD. 2004. The impact of stretching in sports injury risk: a systematic review of the literature. *Medicine and Science in Sports and Exercise.* 36(3):371–78.

Thacker SB, Gilchrist J, Stroup DF, and Kimsey CD. 2002. The prevention of shin splints in sports: a systematic review of literature. *Medicine and Science in Sports and Exercise.* 34(1):32–40.

Thornton GM and Hart DA. 2011. The interface of mechanical loading and biological variables as they pertain to the development of tendinosis. *Journal of Musculoskeletal and Neuronal Interactions.* 11(2):94–105.

Werd MB. 2007. Achilles tendon injuries: a review of classification and treatment. *Journal of the American Podiatric Association.* 97(1):37–48.

Chapter 9

Bear Related Injuries and Fatalities. http://www.nps.gov/yell/naturescience/injuries.htm. Accessed June 10, 2011.

Beckman JP, Lackey CW, and Berger J. 2004. Evaluation of deterrent techniques and dogs to alter behavior of "nuisance" black bears. *Wildlife Society Bulletin.* 32(4):1141–46.

Feldman, D. 2010. Lyme Disease: Challenging Old Stereotypes. http://www.backpackinglight.com/cgi-bin/backpackinglight/lyme_disease_challenging_stereotypes.html. Accessed July 2, 2011.

Fitzgerald KT and Flood AA. 2006. Hymenoptera stings. *Clinical Techniques in Small Animal Practice.* 21:194–204.

Gniadek SJ, Kendall KC. 1998. A summary of bear management in Glacier National Park, Montana, 1960–1994. *Ursus.* 10:155–59.

Herrero S, Higgins A. 2003. Human injuries inflicted by bears in Alberta: 1960–98. *Ursus.* 14(1):44–54.

Herrero S, Higgins A, Cardoza JE, Hajduk LI, and Smith TS. 2011. Fatal attacks by American black bear on people: 1900-2009. *Journal of Wildlife Management.* 75(3):596–603.

Johannes, L. 2009. Deadly dilemma: Do snakebite kits help? *Wall Street Journal.* May 19: page D4.

Jordan R. 2004. Bear Bag Hanging Techniques: A brief review of bear bag hanging techniques with a focus on minimizing weight and maximizing simplicity. http://www.backpackinglight.com/cgi-bin/backpackinglight/bear_bag_hanging_technique.html. Accessed June 25, 2011.

Langley RL, Morrow WE. 1997. Deaths resulting from animal attacks in the United States. *Wilderness and Environmental Medicine.* 8:8–16.

Langley RL. 2005. Animal-related fatalities in the United States—an update. *Wilderness and Environmental Medicine.* 16:67–74.

Sicherer SH, Simmons ER. 2005. Quandaries in prescribing an emergency action plan and self-injectable epinephrine for first-aid management for anaphylaxis in the community. *Journal of Allergy and Clinical Immunology.* 115(3): 575–83.

Sierra Nevada Wilderness Food Storage Requirements. 2008. http://sierrawild.gov/bears/food-storage-map. Accessed June 25, 2011.

Spiller HA, Bosse GM, and Ryan ML. 2010. Use of antivenom for snakebites reported to United States poison centers. *American Journal of Emergency Medicine.* 28:780–85.

United States Department of Agriculture: Agriculture Research Service. Potential United States range expansion of the invasive fire ant. http://www.ars.usda.gov/research/docs.htm?docid=9165&page=15. Accessed July 4, 2011.

Index

Achilles tendon, 101–102, 124
ALDHA Guide, 96
allergic reactions, 167
anaphylactic reactions, 167
animal-related fatalities: bears,
  160–161; bees, hornets,
  wasps, 167; snakes, spiders,
  scorpions, 170
animals, water contamination
  from, 52–54. *See also specific
  types of animals*
ankles: footwear to protect, 26;
  strengthening, 113
ants, 169–170
Appalachian Long Distance Hikers
  Association, 17
Appalachian Trail, 149; completion,
  time for, 145; completion rate,
  xii, xiii; non-completion,
  reasons for, 100, 149; resupply
  options, 96; shelter on the, 74;
  water on the, 53
Appalachian Trail Conservancy, xii
Appalachian Trail thru-hikers:
  injuries, 101, 117; money spent
  by, 175–176; tick bites, 172
*Appalachian Trail Thru-Hiker's
  Companion*, 17
athlete's foot (*tinea pedis*), 134

backpacks. *See also* pack space; pack
  weight: convenience packing,
  120; load distribution, 120; mice
  and, 168; proper fit vs. injury,
  106–108, 119–120
bacteria: basics, 51; Lyme disease
  caused by, 173

bacteria, water treatment options
  for: chemical additives, 63, 64,
  65, 66; filtration, 58, 59, 61;
  mixed oxidants, 67; UV light,
  68, 71
bacteria removed with, 71
batteries, 69
bear bags, 164
bear canisters, 163, 168
bears, 159–165
bear spray, 161–162
bees, 167
bivys, 74, 82–83
blisters: caring for, 135–138;
  footwear and, 23, 24, 26, 118;
  moisture buildup and, 137
boots, 24–26, 151
boredom, managing, 8, 141–145
Borrelia burgdorferi, 173
bounce boxes, 93, 94–95
breaks, taking: in cold, wet weather,
  152; in hot weather, 154; injury
  and, 122–123
bugs. *See specific types of*
Bushbuddy Ultra woodstove, 45

campfire bans, 42, 47
CDT Handbook, 96
chafing, 131–135
chemical additives for water
  treatment: advantages/
  disadvantages, 61–62; chlorine
  bleach, 62–63; chlorine dioxide,
  64–65; iodine, 50, 65–66;
  technology comparison
  chart, 72
chlorine bleach for water treatment,
  62–63, 72

frame of mind: boredom, 141–145;
expectations and, 186; food
and, 4–6, 8, 144; friends and,
143; frustration, 145–146;
impatience, 145–146; luxury
items and, 144–145; music as
an aid to, 142–143; physical
discomfort and, 140–141;
side trips and, 143; solitude
requirements for, 188; success
and, 139–140
friction blisters, 136–138
friends and frame of mind, 143
frustration, managing, 145–146

gear. *See also specific types of*: bears
and, 163–164; choosing, basics
of, 21, 23; costs of, 177; insect
repellent for, 166; replacement
and repair costs, 177
Giardia lamblia, 51
gloves, 151
Gore-Tex, trail runners and, 151
gravity filtration, 50–51, 58–59, 72
ground pads, 91–92
guidebooks, water in, 17–18

hammocks, 75, 83–85
hands, keeping warm and dry, 151
hand sanitizer, 56, 135, 173
hats, 151, 153
health risks from water treatment,
62, 63, 65, 66, 67, 71
heel lifts, constructing, 126
hiker boxes, 94, 96
hornets, 167
hot spots, 136–137
hot weather, 153–154
hunger, 2–5
hydration, need for: clothing and,
19; in cold, wet weather, 152;
in hot weather, 153; terrain
and, 18–19
hygiene: digestive illness and,
56; skin injury and, 135; tick
bites, 173

ibuprofen, 124, 127
illness, waterborne, 51–56
impact blisters, 136, 138
injury. *See also* repetitive stress
injury; skin injury: bear attacks,
160–162; boots and, 111; healing
time, 117; thru-hikers, 101, 117
inline filters, 60–61, 72
insect repellents, 166, 172
insects. *See specific types of*
iodine for water treatment, 65–66, 72

jock itch (*tinea cruris*), 132, 134

knees, reducing injury to, 123

leggings, 151
loneliness, managing, 143–144
long-distance hiking. *See also* thru-
hikers: age distribution, xiii;
barriers to, xii; completion
rates, xii, 21; etiquette, 15–16,
74; non-completion, reasons
for, 100, 149, 175; physical
requirements, xii; resupply,
1–2, 93–97; thrill of, xii;
walking pace, average, 145
Lyme disease, 171

mail drops, 93, 95
maps, 16–18, 156
medications: for bee stings, 167;
for pain relief, 124, 127; for
skin injury, 132
mice, 164, 167–169
mileage: average, 108–109, 145;
injury and, 108–110, 122–123
minimalist (barefoot type) footwear,
26–27
MIOX, 67
mixed oxidants for water treatment,
67, 72

12/13